AAT

Indirect Tax FA 2018

Level 3

Advanced Diploma in

Accounting

Question Bank

For assessments from

January to December 2019

Third edition 2018

ISBN 9781 5097 1876 4

British Library Cataloguing-in-Publication Data

A catalogue record for this book is available from the British Library

Published by

BPP Learning Media Ltd
BPP House, Aldine Place
142-144 Uxbridge Road
London W12 8AA

www.bpp.com/learningmedia

Printed in the United Kingdom

Your learning materials, published by BPP Learning Media Ltd, are printed on paper obtained from traceable sustainable sources.

Contents

Introduction

This is BPP Learning Media's AAT Question Bank for *Indirect Tax*. It is part of a suite of ground-breaking resources produced by BPP Learning Media for AAT assessments.

This Question Bank has been written in conjunction with the BPP Course Book, and has been carefully designed to enable students to practise all of the learning outcomes and assessment criteria for the units that make up *Indirect Tax*. It is fully up to date as at August 2018 and reflects both the AAT's qualification specification and the sample assessment provided by the AAT. All questions are based on the Finance Act 2018, which is examinable to December 2019.

This Question Bank contains these key features:

- Tasks corresponding to each chapter of the Course Book. Some tasks are designed for learning purposes, others are of assessment standard.

- AAT's AQ2016 sample assessment 1 and answers for *Indirect Tax* and further BPP practice assessments. (The AAT sample assessment included in the Question Bank is a draft version. The AAT reserves the right to change the material.)

The emphasis in all tasks and assessments is on the practical application of the skills acquired.

VAT

You may find tasks throughout this Question Bank that need you to calculate or be aware of a rate of VAT. This is stated at 20% in these examples and questions.

Approaching the assessment

When you sit the assessment it is very important that you follow the on screen instructions. This means you need to carefully read the instructions, both on the introduction screens and during specific tasks.

When you access the assessment you should be presented with an introductory screen with information similar to that shown below (taken from the introductory screen from one of the AAT's AQ2016 sample assessments for *Indirect Tax*).

We have provided this **practice assessment** to help you familiarise yourself with our e-assessment environment. It is designed to demonstrate as many of the question types that you may find in a live assessment as possible. It is not designed to be used on its own to determine whether you are ready for a live assessment.

At the end of this practice assessment you will receive an immediate result.

Assessment information:

You have **90 minutes** to complete this practice assessment.

This assessment contains **8 tasks** and you should attempt to complete every task.
Each task is independent. You will not need to refer to your answers in previous tasks.
Read every task carefully to make sure you understand what is required.

Where the date is relevant, it is given in the task data.

Never use minus signs or brackets to indicate negative numbers **unless** task instructions say otherwise.

You must use a full stop to indicate a decimal point.
For example, write 100.57 NOT 100,57 or 100 57

You may use a comma to indicate a number in the thousands, but you don't have to.
For example, 10000 and 10,000 are both acceptable.

If your answer requires rounding, apply normal mathematical rounding rules **unless** the task instructions say otherwise. If your answer is a calculation of VAT and requires rounding, apply the relevant VAT rounding rules.

The actual instructions will vary depending on the subject you are studying for. It is very important you read the instructions on the introductory screen and apply them in the assessment. You don't want to lose marks when you know the correct answer just because you have not entered it in the right format.

In general, the rules set out in the AAT sample assessments for the subject you are studying for will apply in the real assessment, but you should carefully read the information on this screen again in the real assessment, just to make sure. This screen may also confirm the VAT rate used if applicable.

BPP
LEARNING MEDIA

A full stop is needed to indicate a decimal point. We would recommend using minus signs to indicate negative numbers and leaving out the comma signs to indicate thousands, as this results in a lower number of key strokes and less margin for error when working under time pressure. Having said that, you can use whatever is easiest for you as long as you operate within the rules set out for your particular assessment.

You have to show competence throughout the assessment and you should therefore complete all of the tasks. Don't leave questions unanswered.

In some assessments, written or complex tasks may be human marked. In this case you are given a blank space or table to enter your answer into. You are told in the assessments which tasks these are (note: there may be none if all answers are marked by the computer).

If these involve calculations, it is a good idea to decide in advance how you are going to lay out your answers to such tasks by practising answering them on a word document, and certainly you should try all such tasks in this Question Bank and in the AAT's environment using the sample assessment.

When asked to fill in tables, or gaps, never leave any blank even if you are unsure of the answer. Fill in your best estimate.

Note that for some assessments where there is a lot of scenario information or tables of data provided (eg tax tables), you may need to access these via 'pop-ups'. Instructions will be provided on how you can bring up the necessary data during the assessment.

Finally, take note of any task specific instructions once you are in the assessment. For example you may be asked to enter a date in a certain format or to enter a number to a certain number of decimal places.

Grading

To achieve the qualification and to be awarded a grade, you must pass all the mandatory unit assessments, all optional unit assessments (where applicable) and the synoptic assessment.

The AAT Level 3 Advanced Diploma in Accounting will be awarded a grade. This grade will be based on performance across the qualification. Unit assessments and synoptic assessments are not individually graded. These assessments are given a mark that is used in calculating the overall grade.

How overall grade is determined

You will be awarded an overall qualification grade (Distinction, Merit, and Pass). If you do not achieve the qualification you will not receive a qualification certificate, and the grade will be shown as unclassified.

The marks of each assessment will be converted into a percentage mark and rounded up or down to the nearest whole number. This percentage mark is then weighted according to the weighting of the unit assessment or synoptic assessment within the qualification. The resulting weighted assessment percentages are combined to arrive at a percentage mark for the whole qualification.

Grade definition	Percentage threshold
Distinction	90–100%
Merit	80–89%
Pass	70–79%
Unclassified	0–69%
	Or failure to pass one or more assessment/s

Re-sits

Some AAT qualifications such as the AAT Advanced Diploma in Accounting have restrictions in place for how many times you are able to re-sit assessments. Please refer to the AAT website for further details.

You should only be entered for an assessment when you are well prepared and you expect to pass the assessment.

AAT qualifications

The material in this book may support the following AAT qualifications:

AAT Advanced Diploma in Accounting Level 3 and AAT Advanced Diploma in Accounting at SCQF Level 6.

Supplements

From time to time we may need to publish supplementary materials to one of our titles. This can be for a variety of reasons. From a small change in the AAT unit guidance to new legislation coming into effect between editions.

You should check our supplements page regularly for anything that may affect your learning materials. All supplements are available free of charge on our supplements page on our website at:

www.bpp.com/learning-media/about/students

Improving material and removing errors

There is a constant need to update and enhance our study materials in line with both regulatory changes and new insights into the assessments.

From our team of authors BPP appoints a subject expert to update and improve these materials for each new edition.

Their updated draft is subsequently technically checked by another author and from time to time non-technically checked by a proof reader.

We are very keen to remove as many numerical errors and narrative typos as we can but given the volume of detailed information being changed in a short space of time we know that a few errors will sometimes get through our net.

We apologise in advance for any inconvenience that an error might cause. We continue to look for new ways to improve these study materials and would welcome your suggestions. If you have any comments about this book, please email nisarahmed@bpp.com or write to Nisar Ahmed, AAT Head of Programme, BPP Learning Media Ltd, BPP House, Aldine Place, London W12 8AA.

Question Bank

Chapter 1 – Introduction to VAT

Task 1.1

Black Ltd pays for goods from a supplier, and the amount includes VAT.

Is this amount of VAT to be treated as output VAT or input VAT for Black Ltd?

TICK ONE BOX

	✓
Output tax	
Input tax	

Task 1.2

A VAT-registered retailer buys a product for £100 plus VAT of £20. The retailer sells the product to a member of the public for £125 plus VAT of £25.

Which of the following statements is TRUE?

TICK ONE BOX

	✓
The retailer suffers a net cost of £5 VAT being the difference between its output and input tax on the product.	
The true cost of the product to the retailer is £120.	
The retailer does not bear any of the cost of VAT. The member of the public bears the full cost of £25 VAT.	
The retailer bears a VAT cost of £20 and the member of the public bears a VAT cost of £25.	

Task 1.3

A trader buys a product from a manufacturer for £200 plus VAT of £40. The trader is not VAT-registered. The trader sells the product to a member of the public.

Which of the following statements is TRUE?

TICK ONE BOX

	✓
The true cost of the product to the trader is £200.	
The trader suffers a VAT cost of £40.	
The trader accounts for output VAT of £40 on its purchase from the manufacturer.	
The member of the public suffers a VAT cost of £40.	

Chapter 2 – VAT basics

Task 2.1

Identify which of the following types of supply are deemed to be taxable supplies for VAT purposes.

TICK ONE BOX

	✓
Standard-rated supplies only	
Standard and zero-rated supplies	
Zero-rated and exempt supplies	
All three types of supply	

Task 2.2

Several businesses each purchased goods during a month for £13,500 plus VAT.

Identify whether each of these businesses can or cannot reclaim the input tax on the goods purchased.

TICK ONE BOX FOR EACH BUSINESS

Business	Yes, can reclaim ✓	No, cannot reclaim ✓
Bread Ltd – making only standard-rated supplies		
Soup Ltd – making only exempt supplies		
Marmalade Ltd – making only zero-rated supplies		

Task 2.3

A VAT-registered business making only zero-rated supplies has just paid £100 plus VAT of £20 for goods.

What is the net cost of the goods to the business?

TICK ONE BOX

Cost	✓
£0	
£20	
£100	
£120	

Task 2.4

Jam Ltd is a bus company making only zero-rated supplies.

Which ONE of the following statements is correct in relation to Jam Ltd?

TICK ONE BOX

	Correct
Jam Ltd cannot register for VAT.	
If Jam Ltd is VAT-registered it will make payments to HMRC.	
If Jam Ltd is VAT-registered it will have repayments from HMRC.	

Task 2.5

Bradley's business makes taxable supplies of approximately £30,000 each year. He is considering voluntarily registering for VAT.

Identify whether the following statements are true or false in relation to voluntary registration.

TICK ONE BOX FOR EACH STATEMENT

	True	False
If Bradley's business makes zero-rated supplies, it will be in a VAT repayment position.		
If Bradley makes standard-rated supplies, it will be disadvantageous for non VAT-registered customers.		

Task 2.6

Identify whether the following businesses making taxable supplies need to register for VAT immediately, or monitor turnover and register later.

TICK ONE BOX ON EACH LINE

	Register now	Monitor and register later
An existing business with a total turnover of £6,350 per month for the last 12 months.		
A new business with an expected turnover of £25,000 per month for the next 12 months.		
An existing business with a total turnover of £6,000 per month for the last 12 months. A new contract will bring in additional sales of £86,000, in 10 days' time.		

Task 2.7

Identify whether each of these businesses can VAT or cannot register.

TICK ONE BOX FOR EACH BUSINESS

	Can register	Cannot register
Blackberry Ltd – making only zero-rated supplies		
Raspberry Ltd – making standard-rated and zero-rated supplies		
Loganberry Ltd – making only exempt supplies		
Gooseberry Ltd – making standard-rated and exempt supplies		

Task 2.8

Flan Ltd makes only zero-rated supplies.

Identify whether the following statements are true or false in relation to VAT registration.

TICK ONE BOX FOR EACH STATEMENT

	True	False
Flan Ltd cannot register as it makes only zero-rated supplies.		
Flan Ltd is automatically exempt from registering for VAT.		
Flan Ltd can register for VAT.		
Flan Ltd can apply to HMRC to be exempt from registration.		

Task 2.9

Identify whether the following supplies are included or excluded when considering whether the VAT registration limit has been reached.

TICK ONE BOX ON EACH LINE

	Include	Exclude
Standard-rated supplies		
Zero-rated supplies		
Exempt supplies		

Task 2.10

A VAT-registered trader's sales are looking like they will fall below the deregistration limit.

Complete the sentence below by selecting the appropriate number.

The trader may deregister if:

Taxable turnover in the next	▼	months is expected to fall below the deregistration limit.

Picklist:

3
12
24

Task 2.11

For the purpose of your assessment, which of the following is the deregistration threshold?

TICK ONE BOX

	✓
£85,000	
£83,000	
£150,000	
£1.35 million	

Task 2.12

A business has exceeded the VAT registration limit in the last 12 months for the first time. However, this was because of one unusual contract which is unlikely to be repeated.

Identify whether the following statement is true or false.

TICK ONE BOX

	True	False
The business can apply to HMRC for exception from registration, because the level of taxable supplies was temporary.		

Chapter 3 – Inputs and outputs

Task 3.1

Below are details of two VAT invoices to be issued by a trader who makes only standard-rated supplies.

Insert the figures in the relevant columns, as appropriate.

Invoice number	Net £	VAT £	Gross £
1000325			390.60
1000326	452.92		

Task 3.2

Identify whether input tax can be reclaimed by a VAT-registered business in each of the following circumstances.

TICK ONE BOX ON EACH LINE

Circumstance	Yes, can reclaim ✓	No, cannot reclaim ✓
Input tax incurred entertaining a UK client (meals provided during a meeting)		
Input tax incurred on the purchase of a van for use by a furniture repair business		
Input tax incurred providing meals on a training course for an employee		

Task 3.3

Dish Ltd purchases all of the fuel for cars of the salesmen. The company reclaims the VAT on the fuel purchased. The salesmen also use their cars for private motoring.

Complete the sentence below by selecting the appropriate word.

On the VAT return Dish Ltd must include an amount of	▼	tax to take
account of the private fuel used by salesmen.		

Picklist:

input
output

- -

Task 3.4

A VAT-registered business has made the following purchases:

- A car for use by the sales manager for £14,200 plus VAT
- A van for use by the stores man for £10,500 plus VAT

Identify how much VAT can be reclaimed by the business.

TICK ONE BOX

	✓
Nil	
£2,840.00	
£2,100.00	
£4,940.00	

- -

Task 3.5

Where a registered business makes a mixture of standard-rated, zero-rated and exempt supplies, which of the following statements is correct?

TICK ONE BOX

	✓
All input tax can be reclaimed.	
Only input tax relating to standard-rated supplies can be reclaimed.	
All input tax can be reclaimed provided certain *de minimis* tests are met.	
Only input tax relating to standard and zero-rated supplies can be reclaimed.	
No input tax can be reclaimed.	

Task 3.6

Mohammed has purchased goods from a supplier in another EU country.

Complete the sentence below by selecting the appropriate word.

This purchase is known as an/a	▼

Picklist:

acquisition.
despatch.
export.
import.

Task 3.7

James is selling goods to a VAT-registered trader in another EU country.

Complete the sentence below by selecting the appropriate word(s).

In order to benefit from zero rating, the customer must provide	▼

Picklist:

evidence of receipt of goods.
his EU VAT-registration number.
his name and business address.
nothing.

Task 3.8

Lucinda is exporting goods to a customer in India, which is outside the EU.

Complete the sentence below by selecting the appropriate word(s).

Goods exported to customers outside the EU must be treated as	▼

Picklist:

exempt.
outside the scope of VAT.
standard-rated.
zero-rated.

Task 3.9

Jones Ltd, a VAT-registered business, which makes standard-rated supplies, imports goods from outside the EU. The imported goods would be standard-rated with VAT of £3,100 if supplied in the UK.

Which one of the following is the net VAT position for Jones Ltd?

TICK ONE BOX

	Correct
VAT payable to HMRC of £3,100	
VAT reclaimed from HMRC of £3,100	
Nil net VAT effect	

Task 3.10

A UK registered business acquires goods from another EU country.

Which ONE of the following statements is correct?

TICK ONE BOX

	✓
As long as the UK business supplies its VAT number to the EU supplier, the goods will be zero-rated and VAT doesn't need to be accounted for.	
The UK business will charge itself output tax for the goods on the VAT return and reclaim input tax on the same return.	
The UK business will pay output tax to HMRC at the point of entry into the UK and reclaim input tax on the next return.	
The EU supplier will charge VAT on the goods and the UK business will be able to reclaim the VAT on its next return.	

Chapter 4 – Accounting for VAT

Task 4.1

Mr Green is a VAT-registered trader making standard-rated, zero-rated and exempt supplies.

Is he required to retain records of the amounts of different categories of supplies for VAT purposes?

TICK ONE BOX ON EACH LINE

	Yes	No
Standard-rated supplies		
Zero-rated supplies		
Exempt supplies		

Task 4.2

A VAT-registered trader is required to keep adequate records to calculate the VAT due or reclaimable.

Complete the sentence below by inserting the appropriate number from the picklist.

VAT records should usually be retained for	▼	year(s).

Picklist:

1
2
6
20

Task 4.3

Mrs Violet is VAT-registered and runs a business making both cash and credit sales and purchases.

In order to calculate the correct amount of output tax for Mrs Violet's business, which of the following accounting records will be needed?

TICK ONE BOX ON EACH LINE

	Yes	No
Sales day book		
Purchases day book		
Cash receipts book		
Cash payments book		

....

Task 4.4

Mrs Orange is VAT-registered and runs a business making both cash and credit sales and purchases.

In order to calculate the correct amount of input tax for Mrs Orange's business, which of the following accounting records will be needed?

TICK ONE BOX ON EACH LINE

	Yes	No
Sales day book		
Purchases day book		
Cash receipts book		
Cash payments book		
Sales returns day book		
Purchases returns day book		

....

Task 4.5

Complete the sentence below by inserting the appropriate word from the picklist.

A trader must retain a valid VAT	▼	in order to reclaim input tax.

Picklist:

invoice
purchase order

▪▪▪

Task 4.6

Identify which of the following details would not need to appear on a simplified or less detailed VAT invoice for a sale of less than £250.00.

TICK ONE BOX

	✓
The supplier's name and address	
The date of supply	
Description of the goods/ services	
The total excluding VAT	

▪▪▪

Task 4.7

Clipper Ltd holds the following invoices from suppliers.

(a)

VAT reg no 446 9989 57			Jupiter plc
Date: 4 January 20X0			1 London Road
Tax point: 4 January 20X0			Reading
Invoice no.			RL3 7CM
Clippers Ltd			
13 Gale Road			
Chester-le-Street			
NE1 1LB			

Sales of goods

Type	Quantity	VAT rate	Net
		%	£
Earrings @ £0.5 per unit	2,700	20	1,350.00
Earring studs @ £0.5 per unit	2,800	20	1,400.00
			2,750.00
VAT at 20%			550.00
Payable within 60 days			3,300.00
Price if paid within 10 days (net of 5% discount)			2,612.50
VAT at 20%			522.50
Payable within 10 days			3,135.00

(b)

HILLSIDE LTD

'The Glasgow Based Supplier of Quality Jewellery Items'

VAT reg no 337 4849 26

Clipper Ltd

13 Gale Road

Chester-le-Street

NE1 1LB

Invoice no. 0010

Date: 10 August 20X0

Tax point: 10 August 20X0

	£
Sale of 4,000 Jewellery boxes @ £2 per unit	8,000
VAT at 20%	1,600
Total	9,600

Terms: strictly net 30 days

(c)

GENEROUS PLC

11 Low Fell

Leeds

LS1 XY2

Clipper Ltd

13 Gale Road

Chester-le-Street

NE1 1LB

Invoice no: 2221

Date: 12 December 20X0

Tax point: 12 December 20X0

	Net £	VAT £	Total £
4,000 Earrings @ £0.5 per unit	2,000.00	400.00	2,400.00
8,000 Brooches @ £0.3125 per unit	2,500.00	500.00	3,000.00
2,500 'How to make Jewellery' books @ £2 per book	5,000.00	0.00	5,000.00
	9,500.00	900.00	10,400.00

(d)

JEWELS & CO

101 High Street, Gateshead NE2 22P

VAT reg no 499 3493 27

Date: 2 February 20X0

30 necklaces sold for £4 each totalling £120.00 including VAT at 20%.

For each of the above invoices, state whether it is a valid VAT invoice. If it is not valid identify the missing item(s).

Invoice	Valid ✓	Not valid ✓	Missing item(s)
(a)			▼
(b)			▼
(c)			▼
(d)			▼

Picklist:

Applicable rates of VAT (0% & 20%)
Invoice number
Supplier's address
Supplier's VAT registration number

··

Task 4.8

Identify which one of the following statements would need to appear on a pro forma invoice.

TICK ONE BOX

	✓
This is a pro forma invoice.	
This is not a VAT invoice.	
This invoice does not allow input VAT recovery.	
These goods have not yet been delivered.	

··

Task 4.9

Mr Glass has sent a credit note to a customer.

As a result of issuing this credit note, will Mr Glass have to pay more or less VAT to HMRC?

TICK ONE BOX

	✓
More VAT payable	
Less VAT payable	

Task 4.10

Miss Spoon has received a credit note from a supplier.

Which ONE of the following is the effect on VAT?

TICK ONE BOX

	✓
Output tax will increase.	
Output tax will decrease.	
Input tax will increase.	
Input tax will decrease.	

Task 4.11

An invoice is dispatched to a customer on 13 August and the goods are delivered the following day.

What is the tax point in this situation and is it a basic tax point or an actual tax point?

TICK ONE BOX

	✓
13 August and actual tax point	
13 August and basic tax point	
14 August and actual tax point	
14 August and basic tax point	

BPP
LEARNING MEDIA

Task 4.12

A customer orders goods on 13 August. The goods are delivered on 15 August and the invoice is sent to the customer on 31 August. Payment for the goods is made on 15 September.

What is the tax point of this transaction?

TICK ONE BOX

	✓
13 August	
15 August	
31 August	
15 September	

Task 4.13

Below are details of the VAT exclusive (net) amounts on two VAT invoices to be issued by a trader who makes only standard-rated supplies (at 20%).

Invoice 25 – Standard-rated goods sold for £220.00 less a trade discount of 10%.

Invoice 26 – Goods sold for £200.00 with a settlement discount of 3% offered. The trader has chosen to invoice the discounted value.

Insert the figures in the relevant columns, as appropriate.

	Shown on invoice as	
Invoice number	VAT exclusive £	VAT £
25		
26		

Task 4.14

Knife Ltd has not been paid by a customer for an invoice issued some time ago. The company now wishes to claim a refund of the VAT on that invoice from HMRC. It can do so provided certain conditions are fulfilled.

Which one of the following is NOT a relevant condition?

TICK ONE BOX

	✓
Six months must have elapsed since payment was due.	
Output tax has been accounted for and paid.	
Notice must have been received from the customer's liquidators to state that it is insolvent.	
The debt must have been written-off in the accounts of Knife Ltd.	

Chapter 5 – The VAT return

Task 5.1

It is important for a VAT-registered trader to complete VAT returns regularly.

Complete the sentence below by inserting the appropriate number from the picklist.

VAT-registered traders must usually complete a VAT return every	▼	months.

Picklist:

3
6
9
36

Task 5.2

If input tax is greater than output tax in the VAT account, what will this result in?

TICK ONE BOX

	✓
A VAT payment due to HMRC	
A VAT repayment from HMRC	

Task 5.3

Cordelia's business has sales of approximately £200,000. She submits her VAT returns online and pays by BACS.

(a) By what date should the VAT return to 31 May 20X0 be submitted?

TICK ONE BOX

	✓
30 June 20X0	
7 July 20X0	
10 July 20X0	

(b) By what date should any tax due for the return to 31 May 20X0 be paid?

TICK ONE BOX

	✓
30 June 20X0	
7 July 20X0	
10 July 20X0	

Task 5.4

Charlotte's business has sales of approximately £200,000. She submits her VAT returns online and pays her VAT by direct debit.

(a) By what date should the VAT return to 31 May 20X0 be submitted?

TICK ONE BOX

	✓
30 June 20X0	
7 July 20X0	
10 July 20X0	

(b) By what date would any tax due for the return to 31 May 20X0 be paid?

TICK ONE BOX

	✓
30 June 20X0	
7 July 20X0	
10 July 20X0	

Task 5.5

Happy Ltd is able to reclaim bad debt relief on an unpaid invoice.

(a) **Which ONE of the following statements is correct?**

TICK ONE BOX

	✓
Input tax reclaimable will be increased and the bad debt VAT will be included in box 4 on the VAT return.	
Output tax payable will be decreased and the bad debt will VAT be included as a deduction in box 1 on the VAT return.	

Unhappy Ltd reclaims all the input tax on petrol provided to an employee for both business and private use, and will account for the private element of this by using the fuel scale charge.

(b) **Which ONE of the following statements is correct?**

TICK ONE BOX

	✓
Output tax payable will be increased and the fuel scale charge will be included in box 1 on the VAT return.	
Input tax reclaimable will be decreased and the fuel scale charge will be included as a deduction in box 4 on the VAT return.	

Task 5.6

The following accounts have been extracted from the business ledgers.

Sales account

Date 20XX	Reference	Debit £	Date 20XX	Reference	Credit £
			1.10–31.12	Sales day book – UK sales	9,000.00
			1.10–31.12	Sales day book – EU despatches	3,550.00
31.12	Balance c/d	27,600.00	1.10–31.12	Cash book – UK sales	15,050.00
	Total	27,600.00		Total	27,600.00

Purchases and purchases returns account

Date 20XX	Reference	Debit £	Date 20XX	Reference	Credit £
1.10–31.12	Purchases day book – UK purchases	2,250.00	1.10–31.12	Purchases returns day book – UK purchases	975.00
1.10–31.12	Purchases day book – EU acquisitions	4,700.00	31.12	Balance c/d	5,975.00
	Total	6,950.00		Total	6,950.00

VAT account

Date 20XX	Reference	Debit £	Date 20XX	Reference	Credit £
1.10–31.12	Purchases day book	450.00	1.10–31.12	Sales day book	1,800.00
			1.10–31.12	Cash book – UK sales	3,010.00
			1.10–31.12	Purchases returns day book – UK purchases	195.00

The business's EU acquisitions are goods that would normally be standard-rated.

EU despatches are to VAT-registered customers.

(a) Complete the following:

The figure for VAT due on EU acquisitions is:	£	

(b) Complete the following:

The figure for box 1 of the VAT return is:	£	

(c) Complete the following:

The figure for box 4 of the VAT return is:	£	

Task 5.7

The following accounts have been extracted from a business's ledgers for quarter ended 30 June 20X1.

Sales day book summary

	Zero-rated sales	Standard-rated sales	VAT	Total
UK sales	17,000.00	29,500.00	5,900.00	52,400.00

Sales returns day book summary

	Standard-rated sales	VAT	Total
UK sales	2,500.00	500.00	3,000.00

Purchases day book summary

	Standard-rated purchases	VAT on UK purchases	EU purchases	Total
UK purchases/expenses	13,225.00	2,645.00	2,140.00	18,010.00

Purchases returns day book summary

	Standard-rated purchases	VAT	Total
UK purchases	1,700.00	340.00	2,040.00

In June 20X1 a bad debt was written off as irrecoverable in the business's accounting records. The debt was for £720 (VAT-inclusive) on an invoice dated 27 November 20X0. Payment terms for the business are strictly 30 days from date of invoice.

The EU acquisitions are goods that would normally be standard-rated.

Complete boxes 1 to 9 of the VAT return below for quarter ended 30.06.20X1.

VAT return for quarter ended 30.6.20X1		£
VAT due in this period on **sales** and other outputs	**Box 1**	
VAT due in this period on **acquisitions** from other **EC Member States**	**Box 2**	
Total VAT due **(the sum of boxes 1 and 2)**	**Box 3**	
VAT reclaimed in the period on **purchases** and other inputs, including acquisitions from the EC	**Box 4**	
Net VAT to be paid to HM Revenue & Customs or reclaimed by you **(difference between boxes 3 and 4)**	**Box 5**	
Total value of **sales** and all other outputs excluding any VAT. **Include your box 8 figure**	**Box 6**	
Total value of purchases and all other inputs excluding any VAT. **Include your box 9 figure**	**Box 7**	
Total value of all **supplies** of goods and related costs, excluding any VAT, to other **EC Member States**	**Box 8**	
Total value of all **acquisitions** of goods and related costs, excluding any VAT, from other **EC Member States**	**Box 9**	

Chapter 6 – VAT schemes for small businesses

Task 6.1

Declan has heard that there is a special scheme available to some businesses that requires only one VAT return to be prepared each year.

Complete the sentences below by selecting/inserting the appropriate words/number.

Businesses submit only one return each year if they operate the	▼	scheme.

Picklist:

annual accounting
cash accounting
flat rate

To join, taxable supplies in the next 12 months must be below £	▼

Picklist:

150,000
230,000
1,350,000
1,600,000

Task 6.2

Complete the sentence below by selecting the appropriate words.

A business gets automatic bad debt relief if it operates the	▼	scheme.

Picklist:

annual accounting
cash accounting
flat rate

BPP
LEARNING MEDIA

Task 6.3

Harry operates the flat rate scheme for his business.

Complete the sentence below by selecting the appropriate word.

Harry's VAT payable is calculated as a percentage of the VAT	▼	turnover.

Picklist:

exclusive
inclusive

Task 6.4

Debbie has a business with a year ended 30 April 20X0. Debbie operates the annual accounting scheme.

Which one of the following statements is correct?

TICK ONE BOX

	✓
She pays some of her VAT by monthly instalments with the balance due by 31 May 20X0.	
She pays some of her VAT by monthly instalments with the balance due by 30 June 20X0.	
She pays all of her VAT in a single payment by 31 May 20X0.	
She pays all of her VAT in a single payment by 30 June 20X0.	

Task 6.5

Donald operates the cash accounting scheme.

Identify whether the following statements are true or false in relation to the cash accounting scheme.

TICK ONE BOX ON EACH LINE

	True	False
VAT is accounted for on the basis of cash paid and received rather than on invoices.		
The scheme is advantageous for businesses making only zero-rated supplies.		
Businesses must leave the scheme if taxable supplies in the previous 12 months exceed £1,350,000.		

Task 6.6

Jack operates the flat rate scheme.

Identify whether the following statements are true or false in relation to the flat rate scheme.

TICK ONE BOX ON EACH LINE

	True	False
Businesses issue normal VAT invoices to customers.		
VAT is paid in instalments.		
The flat rate percentage applied always depends on the type of business.		
Less VAT may be payable by Jack as a result of operating the scheme.		

Task 6.7

Would a business that gives its customers long periods of credit, but pays its suppliers promptly benefit from operating under the cash accounting scheme?

TICK ONE BOX

	✓
Yes, because output VAT would be paid later and input VAT would be reclaimed at the same time or earlier.	
No, because input VAT would be reclaimed later and output VAT would be paid at the same time or earlier.	

Task 6.8

Alex is a VAT registered trader who operates the flat rate scheme. He is defined as a 'limited cost trader'.

His sales for the quarter ended 31 March 2019 are as follows:

Standard-rated	£18,000 (net)
Zero-rated	£12,000

He also acquired the following fixed assets in the period:

Computer equipment costing	£1,200 (net)
Shop fittings costing	£3,000 (net)

What is Alex's VAT payable for the quarter?

TICK ONE BOX

	✓
£5,544.00	
£4,950.00	
£4,944.00	
£4,704.00	

Task 7.1

You have discovered an error on the VAT return of a client.

You adjust for this error on the next VAT return if it is which of the following?

TICK ONE BOX

	✓
More than the error correction reporting threshold, but not deliberate	
Less than the error correction reporting threshold and not deliberate	
More than the error correction reporting threshold and was deliberate	
Less than the error correction reporting threshold, but was deliberate	

Task 7.2

Amy's business has made a large error that exceeded the error correction reporting threshold, but was not careless or deliberate.

Identify whether the following statements are true or false in relation to this large error.

TICK ONE BOX

	True	False
Amy can adjust this on her next return.		
Amy cannot adjust this error on her next return and will be liable for a penalty.		

Task 7.3

A business has made a small understatement of input tax in a previous quarter that is below the error correction threshold.

Should this adjustment be shown on the latest VAT return, and if so where on the return?

TICK ONE BOX

	✓
No – not shown on the return	
Yes – shown in box 1	
Yes – shown in box 4	

Task 7.4

Abdul has just submitted his VAT return late. He has previously sent in all VAT returns on time.

For the purpose of your assessment, which one of the following statements is correct?

TICK ONE BOX

	✓
No action will be taken by HMRC.	
HMRC will issue a surcharge liability notice.	
HMRC will issue a surcharge liability notice and charge a penalty.	
HMRC charge a penalty only.	

Task 7.5

Complete the sentence below by selecting the appropriate number.

A business has a requirement to retain VAT records for	▼	years.

Picklist:

three
four
six
ten

Task 7.6

Tax avoidance is illegal and consists of seeking to pay too little tax by deliberately misleading HMRC.

Decide whether this statement is true or false.

TICK ONE BOX

	✓
True	
False	

Task 7.7

Your client is Howard, who is currently VAT-registered. Howard's business is affected by a change in the VAT registration limits. Until now your client has had to be VAT-registered. However, the business has slowed down and the VAT registration/deregistration limits have increased. As a result your client could choose to deregister. The majority of the client's customers are members of the general public and not VAT-registered.

Assume today's date is 1 June 20X0.

Draft an email to your client advising him of the options available to him.

To: [_____ ▼] (1)

From: [_____ ▼] (2)

Date: [_____ ▼] (3)

Subject: [_____ ▼] (4)

Please be advised that the current level of your business turnover is such that you are able to VAT [_____ ▼] (5) As you will no longer need to charge [_____ ▼] (6) VAT to your customers, there are two options open to you.

1. Your selling prices can decrease to the VAT-exclusive amount

    As a result your profits will [_____ ▼] (7) At the same time your

    customer will have [_____ ▼] (8) cost.

2. Your selling prices can stay at the same VAT-inclusive amount

    As a result your profits will [_____ ▼] (9) At the same time your

    customer will have [_____ ▼] (10) cost.

If you wish to discuss this further please feel free to make an appointment.

Kind regards

Picklist:

(1)   Howard / AN Accountant
(2)   Howard / AN Accountant
(3)   1 June 20X0 / 31 March 20X0
(4)   VAT rates / VAT deregistration
(5)   register. / deregister.
(6)   input / output
(7)   increase. / decrease. / stay the same.
(8)   the same / a higher / a lower
(9)   increase. / decrease. / stay the same.
(10) the same / a higher / a lower

Task 7.8

It is 1 October 20X0 and you work for a firm of accountants, ABC & Co. Your client Mr Jones is considering joining the annual accounting scheme. Mr Jones's business operates from Unit 1 Alias Industrial Estate, Chelmsford, Essex, CM2 3FG.

You have been asked to complete the letter to Mr Jones explaining how the annual accounting scheme operates.

ABC & Co
2 Smith Street
London
W1 2DE

1 October 20X0

Mr Jones
Unit 1 Alias Industrial Estate
Chelmsford
Essex
CM2 3FG

Dear [▾] (1)

[▾] (2) **(subject)**

Further to our telephone conversation of today, I have set out below the details relating to the annual accounting scheme.

Your business can join the annual accounting scheme if the value of its taxable supplies [▾] (3) VAT, in the forthcoming [▾] (4) months does not exceed £ [▾] (5)

Under this scheme the business usually makes [_____ ▼] (6) equal monthly instalments. Each of these instalments is [_____ ▼] (7) of the prior year VAT liability. The first payment is due at the [_____ ▼] (8) of the [_____ ▼] (9) month of the accounting period.

The balancing payment and the VAT return will be sent to HMRC within [_____ ▼] (10) of the end of the accounting period.

I hope that this has clarified the position. If you wish to discuss this further please do not hesitate to contact me.

Yours sincerely

Picklist:

(1)   Mr Jones / ABC & Co
(2)   Annual accounting scheme / Cash accounting scheme
(3)   including / excluding
(4)   3 / 12
(5)   150,000 / 1,350,000 / 1,600,000
(6)   four / nine / ten
(7)   ¼ / 1/10
(8)   beginning / end
(9)   first / third / fourth
(10) 30 days / a month and seven days / two months

Answer Bank

Chapter 1

Task 1.1

	✓
Output tax	
Input tax	✓

Task 1.2

	✓
The retailer suffers a net cost of £5 VAT being the difference between its output and input tax on the product.	
The true cost of the product to the retailer is £120.	
The retailer does not bear any of the cost of VAT. The member of the public bears the full cost of £25 VAT.	✓
The retailer bears a VAT cost of £20 and the member of the public bears a VAT cost of £25.	

Provided the retailer makes only taxable supplies, it can recover its input VAT of £20 on its purchase, and so suffers no VAT cost. The cost of the product to the retailer is therefore £100.

The retailer will collect £25 output VAT from the customer and pay it to HMRC but it suffers no VAT cost itself. The member of the public, the final consumer, suffers the full VAT of £25.

Task 1.3

	✓
The true cost of the product to the trader is £200.	
The trader suffers a VAT cost of £40.	✓
The trader accounts for output VAT of £40 on its purchase from the manufacturer.	
The member of the public suffers a VAT cost of £40.	

The trader is not VAT-registered. Therefore, it cannot recover input VAT of £40 on its purchase. The true cost of the product to the trader is therefore £240, the trader suffering the VAT of £40.

The trader does not account for VAT as it is not VAT-registered (and in any case this would be input VAT on the purchase, not output VAT).

The member of the public suffers no VAT, as the trader is not registered, so does not charge any VAT on the sale.

Chapter 2

Task 2.1

	✓
Standard-rated supplies only	
Standard and zero-rated supplies	✓
Zero-rated and exempt supplies	
All three types of supply	

Task 2.2

Business	Yes, can reclaim ✓	No, cannot reclaim ✓
Bread Ltd – making only standard-rated supplies	✓	
Soup Ltd – making only exempt supplies		✓
Marmalade Ltd – making only zero-rated supplies	✓	

Task 2.3

Cost	✓
£0	
£20	
£100	✓
£120	

A VAT-registered trader making zero-rated supplies can recover all its input VAT, and so the cost of the goods is £100.

Task 2.4

	Correct
Jam Ltd cannot register for VAT.	
If Jam Ltd is VAT-registered it will make payments to HMRC.	
If Jam Ltd is VAT-registered it will have repayments from HMRC.	✓

Jam Ltd can recover input tax, but has no output tax (charged at 0%), so will be in a net repayment position.

Task 2.5

	True	False
If Bradley's business makes zero-rated supplies, it will be in a VAT repayment position.	✓	
If Bradley makes standard-rated supplies, it will be disadvantageous for non VAT-registered customers.	✓	

If Bradley makes zero-rated supplies, he can recover his input tax but has no output tax (charged at 0%) so will be in a repayment position.

If Bradley makes standard-rated supplies, he will have to charge VAT at 20%. Non VAT-registered customers cannot recover this, and so the goods will be more expensive to them.

Task 2.6

	Register now	Monitor and register later
An existing business with a total turnover of £6,350 per month for the last 12 months.		✓
A new business with an expected turnover of £25,000 per month for the next 12 months.		✓
An existing business with a total turnover of £6,000 per month for the last 12 months. A new contract will bring in additional sales of £86,000, in 10 days' time.	✓	

The first business has not exceeded the registration threshold of £85,000 in the last 12 months (£6,350 × 12 = £76,200) so does not have to register yet.

The new business has to register once it has exceeded the threshold in the last 12 months (or since starting to trade). It only has to register on the basis of its **expected** turnover, if it is expected to exceed the threshold in the next 30 days alone. This is not the case.

The existing business has not exceeded the threshold in the last 12 months (£6,000 × 12 = £72,000). However the new contract means it will exceed the threshold in the next 30 days alone, and so has to register now under the future test.

Task 2.7

	Can register	Cannot register
Blackberry Ltd – making only zero-rated supplies	✓	
Raspberry Ltd – making standard-rated and zero-rated supplies	✓	
Loganberry Ltd – making only exempt supplies		✓
Gooseberry Ltd – making standard-rated and exempt supplies	✓	

Task 2.8

	True	False
Flan Ltd cannot register as it makes only zero-rated supplies.		✓
Flan Ltd is automatically exempt from registering for VAT.		✓
Flan Ltd can register for VAT.	✓	
Flan Ltd can apply to HMRC to be exempt from registration.	✓	

Flan Ltd is able to register for VAT, and must do so if it exceeds the registration threshold, but it is possible to apply to HMRC so that it does not have to register, as it makes only zero-rated supplies.

••

Task 2.9

	Include	Exclude
Standard-rated supplies	✓	
Zero-rated supplies	✓	
Exempt supplies		✓

••

Task 2.10

Taxable turnover in the next	**12**	months is expected to fall below the deregistration limit.

••

Task 2.11

	✓
£85,000	
£83,000	✓
£150,000	
£1.35 million	

••

Task 2.12

	True	False
The business can apply to HMRC for exception from registration, because the level of taxable supplies was temporary.	✓	

Chapter 3

Task 3.1

Invoice number	Net £	VAT £	Gross £
1000325	325.50	65.10	390.60
1000326	452.92	90.58	543.50

Workings:

£390.60 × 1/6 = £65.10 so net amount = £390.60 – £65.10 = £325.50

£452.92 × 20% = £90.58 so gross amount = £452.92 + £90.58 = £543.50

....

Task 3.2

Circumstance	Yes, can reclaim ✓	No, cannot reclaim ✓
Input tax incurred entertaining a UK client (meals provided during a meeting)		✓
Input tax incurred on the purchase of a van for use by a furniture repair business	✓	
Input tax incurred providing meals on a training course for an employee	✓	

....

Task 3.3

On the VAT return Dish Ltd must include an amount of account of the private fuel used by salesmen.	**output**	tax to take

Output tax in the form of the fuel scale charge must be included.

....

Task 3.4

	✓
Nil	
£2,840.00	
£2,100.00	✓
£4,940.00	

VAT is irrecoverable on cars purchased with both business and private use.

Task 3.5

	✓
All input tax can be reclaimed.	
Only input tax relating to standard-rated supplies can be reclaimed.	
All input tax can be reclaimed provided certain *de minimis* tests are met.	✓
Only input tax relating to standard and zero-rated supplies can be reclaimed.	
No input tax can be reclaimed.	

Task 3.6

This purchase is known as an	**acquisition**.

Task 3.7

In order to benefit from zero rating, the customer must provide	**his EU VAT-registration number**.

Task 3.8

Goods exported to customers outside the EU must be treated as	**zero-rated**.

Task 3.9

	Correct
VAT payable to HMRC of £3,100	
VAT reclaimed from HMRC of £3,100	
Nil net VAT effect	✓

VAT is paid to HMRC at the airport/port and then reclaimed as input tax on the VAT return, so the net effect is the same as a purchase in the UK ie nil net VAT effect.

Task 3.10

	✓
As long as the UK business supplies its VAT number to the EU supplier, the goods will be zero-rated and VAT doesn't need to be accounted for.	
The UK business will charge itself output tax for the goods on its VAT return and reclaim input tax on the same return.	✓
The UK business will pay output tax to HMRC at the point of entry into the UK and reclaim input tax on the next return.	
The EU supplier will charge VAT on the goods and the UK business will be able to reclaim the VAT on its next return.	

The first statement is incorrect as the UK business must account for output tax and reclaim input tax (although the EU supplier would treat the supply as zero-rated).

The third statement is incorrect as this describes the position for an import from outside the EU.

The fourth statement is incorrect as it is the UK business (and not the EU supplier) which must account for the output tax.

Chapter 4

Task 4.1

	Yes	No
Standard-rated supplies	✓	
Zero-rated supplies	✓	
Exempt supplies	✓	

Task 4.2

VAT records should usually be retained for	6	year(s).

Task 4.3

	Yes	No
Sales day book	✓	
Purchases day book		✓
Cash receipts book	✓	
Cash payments book		✓

Task 4.4

	Yes	No
Sales day book		✓
Purchases day book	✓	
Cash receipts book		✓
Cash payments book	✓	
Sales returns day book		✓
Purchases returns day book	✓	

Task 4.5

A trader must retain a valid VAT	**invoice**	in order to reclaim input tax.

Task 4.6

	✓
The supplier's name and address	
The date of supply	
Description of the goods/ services	
The total excluding VAT	✓

For each applicable VAT rate the total including VAT is required together with the rates.

Task 4.7

Invoice	Valid ✓	Not valid ✓	Missing item(s)
(a)		✓	Invoice number
(b)		✓	Supplier's address
(c)		✓	Supplier's VAT registration number/ Applicable rates of VAT (0% & 20%)
(d)	✓		

Note.

The total value of the supply by Jewels & Co, including VAT, does not exceed £250, so a less detailed invoice is permissible.

The invoice is valid, because it includes all the information which must be shown on a less detailed invoice.

Task 4.8

	✓
This is a pro forma invoice.	
This is not a VAT invoice.	✓
This invoice does not allow input VAT recovery.	
These goods have not yet been delivered.	

Task 4.9

	✓
More VAT payable	
Less VAT payable	✓

The credit note will decrease the output tax, and so less VAT will be payable.

Task 4.10

	✓
Output tax will increase.	
Output tax will decrease.	
Input tax will increase.	
Input tax will decrease.	✓

Task 4.11

	✓
13 August and actual tax point	✓
13 August and basic tax point	
14 August and actual tax point	
14 August and basic tax point	

The basic tax point is 14 August, the date of delivery of the goods, but the invoice date is before this, so the tax point is an actual tax point of 13 August.

Task 4.12

	✓
13 August	
15 August	✓
31 August	
15 September	

The basic tax point is 15 August, the date of delivery of the goods, and the invoice is issued more than 14 days later, so this does not create an actual tax point.

* *

Task 4.13

Invoice number	Shown on invoice as:	
	VAT exclusive £	VAT £
25	198.00	39.60
26	194.00*	38.80

* The trader has chosen to invoice the discounted value, and VAT is based on this. A further invoice will be required if the customer chooses not to take up the settlement discount.

Working

£194.00 × 20% = £38.80

* *

Task 4.14

	✓
Six months must have elapsed since payment was due.	
Output tax has been accounted for and paid.	
Notice must have been received from the customer's liquidators to state that it is insolvent.	✓
The debt must have been written-off in the accounts of Knife Ltd.	

* *

Chapter 5

Task 5.1

VAT-registered traders must usually complete a VAT return every	**3**	months.

Task 5.2

	✓
A VAT payment due to HMRC	
A VAT repayment from HMRC	✓

Task 5.3

(a) **VAT return to 31 May 20X0 submission date**

	✓
30 June 20X0	
7 July 20X0	✓
10 July 20X0	

(b) **VAT due**

	✓
30 June 20X0	
7 July 20X0	✓
10 July 20X0	

Task 5.4

(a) **VAT return to 31 May 20X0 submission date**

	✓
30 June 20X0	
7 July 20X0	✓
10 July 20X0	

(b) VAT due

	✓
30 June 20X0	
7 July 20X0	
10 July 20X0	✓

Task 5.5

(a)

	✓
Input tax reclaimable will be increased and the bad debt VAT will be included in box 4 on the VAT return.	✓
Output tax payable will be decreased and the bad debt VAT will be included as a deduction in box 1 on the VAT return.	

(b)

	✓
Output tax payable will be increased and the fuel scale charge will be included in box 1 on the VAT return.	✓
Input tax reclaimable will be decreased and the fuel scale charge will be included as a deduction in box 4 on the VAT return.	

Task 5.6

(a)

The figure for VAT due on EU acquisitions is:	£	940.00

(b)

The figure for box 1 of the VAT return is:	£	4,810.00

VAT due in this period on sales and other outputs = £1,800 + £3,010

(c)

The figure for box 4 of the VAT return is:	£	1,195.00

VAT reclaimed in the period on purchases and other inputs, including acquisitions from the EU = £450 – £195 + £940

Task 5.7

VAT return for quarter ended 30.6.20X1		£
VAT due in this period on **sales** and other outputs	**Box 1**	5,400.00
VAT due in this period on **acquisitions** from other **EC Member States**	**Box 2**	428.00
Total VAT due **(the sum of boxes 1 and 2)**	**Box 3**	5,828.00
VAT reclaimed in the period on **purchases** and other inputs, including acquisitions from the EC	**Box 4**	2,853.00
Net VAT to be paid to HM Revenue & Customs or reclaimed by you **(difference between boxes 3 and 4)**	**Box 5**	2,975.00
Total value of **sales** and all other outputs excluding any VAT. **Include your box 8 figure**	**Box 6**	44,000
Total value of purchases and all other inputs excluding any VAT. **Include your box 9 figure**	**Box 7**	13,665
Total value of all **supplies** of goods and related costs, excluding any VAT, to other **EC Member States**	**Box 8**	0
Total value of all **acquisitions** of goods and related costs, excluding any VAT, from other **EC Member States**	**Box 9**	2,140

Workings: £

Box 1   VAT on sales from the sales day book   5,900.00

            Less: VAT on credit notes   (500.00)

                                                                    5,400.00

Box 2   VAT due on EU acquisitions (2,140 × 20%)   **428.00**

Box 3   Total of box 1 and box 2 £5,400 + £428   **5,828.00**

Box 4   VAT on purchases from purchases day book   2,645.00

            VAT on EU acquisitions   428.00

            Bad debt relief (720.00 × 1/6)   120.00

            Less: VAT on credit notes   (340.00)

                                                                    2,853.00

Box 5   Net VAT due Box 3 minus box 4 £5,828 – £2,853   **2,975.00**

Box 6   Zero-rated credit UK sales   17,000.00

            Standard-rated credit UK sales   29,500.00

            Less: standard-rated credit notes   (2,500.00)

                                                                    44,000

Box 7   Standard-rated credit UK purchases   13,225.00

            EU purchases   2,140.00

            Less: standard-rated credit notes   (1,700.00)

                                                                    13,665

Box 8   EU sales   **0**

Box 9   EU acquisitions   **2,140**

Chapter 6

Task 6.1

Businesses submit only 1 return each year if they operate the	**annual accounting**	scheme.

To join, taxable supplies in the next 12 months must be below £	**1,350,000**

Task 6.2

A business gets automatic bad debt relief if it operates the	**cash accounting**	scheme.

Task 6.3

Harry's VAT payable is calculated as a percentage of the VAT	**inclusive**	turnover.

Task 6.4

	✓
She pays some of her VAT by monthly instalments with the balance due by 31 May 20X0.	
She pays some of her VAT by monthly instalments with the balance due by 30 June 20X0.	✓
She pays all of her VAT in a single payment by 31 May 20X0.	
She pays all of her VAT in a single payment by 30 June 20X0.	

Task 6.5

	True	False
VAT is accounted for on the basis of cash paid and received rather than on invoices.	✓	
The scheme is advantageous for businesses making only zero-rated supplies.		✓*
Businesses must leave the scheme if taxable supplies in the previous 12 months exceed £1,350,000.		✓**

*   Input tax is generally reclaimed later under the cash accounting scheme, so this is not advantageous

**   The limit for leaving is £1,600,000

Task 6.6

	True	False
Businesses issue normal VAT invoices to customers.	✓	
VAT is paid in instalments.		✓
The flat rate percentage applied always depends on the type of business.		✓*
Less VAT may be payable by Jack as a result of operating the scheme.	✓	

* limited cost traders use a flat rate of 16.5% irrespective of the type of business

Task 6.7

	✓
Yes, because output VAT would be paid later and input VAT would be reclaimed at the same time or earlier.	✓
No, because input VAT would be reclaimed later and output VAT would be paid at the same time or earlier.	

Task 6.8

	✓
£5,544.00	
£4,950.00	
£4,944.00	✓
£4,704.00	

Gross total turnover is £(18,000 × 1.2 + 12,000) = £33,600

£33,600 × 16.5% (limited cost trader %) = £5,544

Input tax recoverable on fixed assets costing over £2,000 = 20% × £3,000 = £600

VAT payable is therefore £(5,544-600) = £4,944.00

Chapter 7

Task 7.1

More than the error correction reporting threshold, but not deliberate	
Less than the error correction reporting threshold and not deliberate	✓
More than the error correction reporting threshold and was deliberate	
Less than the error correction reporting threshold, but was deliberate	

Task 7.2

	True	False
Amy can adjust this on her next return.		✓
Amy cannot adjust this error on her next return and will be liable for a penalty.		✓

Amy cannot adjust this error on her next return but there will not be a penalty as it was not careless or deliberate.

Task 7.3

No – not shown on the return	
Yes – shown in box 1	
Yes – shown in box 4	✓

It is shown as an increase in the input tax at box 4 on the VAT return.

Task 7.4

	✓
No action will be taken by HMRC.	
HMRC will issue a surcharge liability notice.	✓
HMRC will issue a surcharge liability notice and charge a penalty.	
HMRC charge a penalty only.	

Task 7.5

A business has a requirement to retain VAT records for	**six**	years.

Task 7.6

	✓
True	
False	✓

Tax avoidance is a way of trying to legally reduce your tax burden, whereas tax evasion is illegal and consists of seeking to pay too little tax by deliberately misleading HMRC.

Task 7.7

To: | **Howard** | (1)
From: | **AN Accountant** | (2)
Date: | **1 June 20X0** | (3)
Subject: | **VAT deregistration** | (4)

Please be advised that the current level of your business turnover is such that you are able to VAT **deregister.** (5) As you will no longer need to charge **output** (6) VAT to your customers, there are two options open to you.

1. Your selling prices can decrease to the VAT-exclusive amount

    As a result your profits will **stay the same.** (7) At the same time your customer will have **a lower** (8) cost.

2. Your selling prices can stay at the same VAT-inclusive amount

    As a result your profits will **increase.** (9) At the same time your customer will have **the same** (10) cost.

If you wish to discuss this further please feel free to make an appointment.

Kind regards

....

Task 7.8

ABC & Co
2 Smith Street
London
W1 2DE

1 October 20X0

Mr Jones
Unit 1 Alias Industrial Estate
Chelmsford
Essex
CM2 3FG

Dear **Mr Jones**

Annual accounting scheme

Further to our telephone conversation of today, I have set out below the details relating to the annual accounting scheme.

Your business can join the annual accounting scheme if the value of its taxable supplies **excluding** VAT, in the forthcoming **12** months does not exceed £ **1,350,000.**

Under this scheme the business usually makes **nine** equal monthly instalments. Each of these instalments is **1/10** of the prior year VAT liability. The first payment is due at the **end** of the **fourth** month of the accounting period.

The balancing payment and the VAT return will be sent to HMRC within **two months** of the end of the accounting period.

I hope that this has clarified the position. If you wish to discuss this further please do not hesitate to contact me.

Yours sincerely

AAT AQ2016 SAMPLE ASSESSMENT 1 INDIRECT TAX FA 2018

Time allowed: 1 hour and 30 minutes

The AAT may call the assessments on their website, under study support resources, either a 'practice assessment' or 'sample assessment'.

AAT AQ2016

SAMPLE ASSESSMENT 1

BPP
LEARNING MEDIA

Indirect Tax FA 2018 (IDRX)
AAT sample assessment 1

Task 1 (6 marks)

A business reached the VAT registration threshold six months ago but did not register for VAT. It has since charged £42,000 to customers for standard-rated taxable supplies.

(a) (i) **How much will the business have to pay HMRC in respect of output tax for its period of non-registration? The business has chosen to treat the amount charged as VAT-inclusive.** **(2 marks)**

£

(ii) **Must the business's customers reimburse the business for the output tax now payable to HMRC?** **(1 mark)**

Drop-down list:

Yes
No

(b) **Complete the following statement by choosing one option.** **(2 marks)**

To find out information about registering on a special scheme for VAT, a business should, first of all, ...

	✓
... call HMRC on the General Enquiries helpline.	
... look at the HMRC website.	
... write to the HMRC.	

(c) **Complete the following statement by choosing one option.** **(1 mark)**

Voluntary registration for VAT is available to any business...

	✓
...with taxable turnover above the registration threshold.	
...that makes at least some taxable supplies.	

Task 2 (9 marks)

A business makes the following purchase:

- Standard-rated goods for £110 plus VAT of £22
- Zero-rated goods for £68.

(a) **Which one of the following amounts must appear on the simplified VAT invoice issued to the business?** **(3 marks)**

	✓
£22	
£68	
£110	
£200	

A business makes the following mixed supply:

standard-rated goods for £185 plus VAT of £37; exempt goods for £28.

(b) **May the business issue a simplified invoice for this sale?**

(1 mark)

	✓
Yes	
No	

A business incurs input tax in relation to its exempt, its zero-rated and its standard-rated supplies. The input tax that it incurs in relation to its exempt supplies is more than the *de minimus* amount.

(c) **Complete the following statement regarding the business's input tax for this period.** **(3 marks)**

The business can reclaim [▼] (1) of its input tax

because it makes [▼] (2)

Drop-down lists:

(1)   some
      none
      all

(2)   exempt supplies that are more than the *de minimus* amount.
      some standard-rated supplies.

A business delivers goods to its customer on 11 February and issues a VAT invoice on 27 February.

(d)   What is the tax point for this supply?   **(1 mark)**

	✓
11 February.	
27 February.	

A business despatches goods to its customer on 15 July.

(e)   What is the latest date by which it can issue a VAT invoice? Select one date from the calendar.   **(1 mark)**

Task 3 (5 marks)

A business operates the annual accounting scheme and always has more output tax than input tax. The end of its VAT period is 30 September.

(a)   Identify whether each of the following statements is true or false.   **(2 marks)**

	True ✓	False ✓
The due date for the VAT return is 31 October.		
Businesses that choose to pay VAT monthly must make at least nine VAT payments in any calendar year.		

A business operates no special accounting schemes. It invoiced a standard-rated supply of £1,500 plus VAT on 1 February offering 1 month credit, but wrote the debt off on 15 June. All the conditions for claiming bad debt relief have been met by the business.

(b)   What is the earliest opportunity for the business to claim bad debt relief?   **(3 marks)**

	✓
In its VAT period ending 31 March.	
In its Vat period ending 30 June.	
In its VAT period ending 30 September.	
In its VAT period ending 31 December.	

Task 4 (9 marks)

A business has just discovered it made the following non-deliberate, non-careless errors that affect its previous VAT return:

- VAT of £56 on an invoice to a UK customer was entered twice in the accounting records.

- VAT £178 on a credit note to a UK customer was omitted from the accounting records.

The business is permitted to correct the net error on its current VAT return.

(a) **Which correction should the business make in Box 1 of its current VAT return?** **(3 marks)**

	✓
Add £122.	
Add £234.	
Deduct £122.	
Deduct £234.	

A large business has a Box 6 figure on its current VAT return of £1,355,000. It has discovered a net error in a previous VAT period of £14,025. It has corrected this error on the current VAT return without separate notification to HMRC.

(b) **Which of the following will be the consequence for the business?** **(2 marks)**

HMRC will regard this as...

	✓
... the correct action so there will be no further consequence.	
... the incorrect action and issue a surcharge liability notice.	
... a deliberate error and issue a penalty.	

(c) **Complete the following statement.** **(2 marks)**

A business's accountant needs to keep up-to-date with changes in VAT regulations and practice to comply with the ethical principle of

[▼] .

Drop-down list:

objectivity.
professional competence.
confidentiality.

(d)   **Identify whether each of the following statements about VAT rules and practice is true or false.**   **(2 marks)**

	True ✓	False ✓
A business which fails to submit a VAT return may have to pay an amount which HMRC assesses to be due.		
A business which receives a surcharge liability notice issued by HMRC must immediately pay a surcharge to HMRC.		

Task 5 (7 marks)

A business supplies a standard-rated item at a price of £780 excluding VAT. The customer pays within 10 days and takes advantage of the 5% prompt payment discount offered for such prompt payment.

(a)   **How much output tax should the business include in its VAT account for this supply?**   **(2 marks)**

£ [   ]

A manufacturer supplies a standard-rated item at a VAT-inclusive price of £520.

(b)   **How much output tax should the manufacturer include in its VAT account for this supply?**   **(2 marks)**

£ [   ]

A business has recorded a credit note from a supplier showing VAT of £96, when it should have been £69. Currently, the business's VAT account shows output tax of £5,490 and input tax of £1,340.

(c)   **When the error is corrected, which one of the following figures will be correct?**   **(3 marks)**

	✓
Input tax £1,313.	
Input tax £1,367.	
Output tax £5,463.	
Output tax £5,517.	

Task 6 (7 marks)

You need to prepare selected figures for a business's VAT return for the period ended 30 April.

The following accounts have been extracted from the ledgers:

Sales account

Date	Reference	Debit £	Date	Reference	Credit £
30/04	Balance c/d	162,456.37	01/02–30/04	Sales day-book – UK sales	137,591.16
			01/02–30/04	Sales day-book – EU despatches	24,865.21
		162,456.37			162,456.37

VAT account

Date	Reference	Debit £	Date	Reference	Credit £
01/02–30/04	Purchases day-book – UK purchases	16,347.09	01/02–30/04	Sales day-book – UK sales	27,518.23
			01/02–30/04	Purchases returns day-book – UK purchases returns	1,774.28

You discover that during the VAT period the business sold a van for £6,240, including VAT of £1,040. It recorded the gross sale in the sales account and made no entry in the VAT account.

The business owner tries to persuade you to ignore this matter.

(a)   Which of the following should be your response to the business owner?   (1 mark)

	✓
If you insist then I will respect your authority and ignore the matter.	
Both VAT regulations and my ethical principles mean I cannot ignore the matter.	

The business owner decides that both the sales account and the VAT account need to be corrected.

BPP LEARNING MEDIA

(b) Calculate the figure to be included in Box 1 of the VAT return, once any necessary corrections to the ledger accounts have been made. **(2 marks)**

£ [   ]

(c) Calculate the figure to be included in Box 4 of the VAT return, once any necessary corrections to the ledger accounts have been made. **(2 marks)**

£ [   ]

(d) Calculate the figure to be included in Box 6 of the VAT return, once any necessary corrections to the ledger accounts have been made. Your figure should be in whole pounds only. **(2 marks)**

£ [   ]

Task 7 (17 marks)

You need to prepare all the figures for completion of a business's online VAT return for the period ended 30 June.

The following accounts have been extracted from the ledgers:

Sales account

Date	Reference	Debit £	Date	Reference	Credit £
30/06	Balance c/d	278,369.14	01/04–30/06	Sales day-book – UK sales	180,916.77
			01/04–30/06	Cash book – UK sales	97,452.37
	Total	278,369.14		Total	278,369.14

Purchases account

Date	Reference	Debit £	Date	Reference	Credit £
01/04–30/06	Purchases day-book – UK purchases	64,974.73	30/06	Balance c/d	101,759.38
01/04–30/06	Purchases day-book – EU acquisitions	36,784.65			
	Total	101,759.38		Total	101,759.38

VAT account

Date	Reference	Debit £	Date	Reference	Credit £
01/04–30/06	Purchases day-book – UK purchases	12,994.94	01/04–30/06	Sales day-book – UK sales	36,183.35
			01/04–30/06	Cash book – UK sales	19,490.47

All the acquisitions were standard-rated goods.

(a) **Enter the relevant figures into the online VAT return for the period ended 30 June. Do not leave any box blank.**

(13 marks)

Online VAT Return for period ended 30 June	
Please note: Enter values in pounds sterling, including pence, for example 1000.00	
VAT due in this period on sales and other outputs. (Box 1)	[ ]
VAT due in this period on acquisitions from other EC member states. (Box 2)	[ ]
Total VAT due (the sum of boxes 1 and 2). (Box 3)	**Calculated value**
VAT reclaimed in the period on purchases and other inputs (including acquisitions from the EC). (Box 4)	[ ]
Net VAT to be paid to HM Revenue & Customs or reclaimed by you (difference between boxes 3 and 4). (Box 5)	**Calculated value**
Total value of sales and all other outputs including any VAT. Include your Box 8 figure. (Box 6)	[ ] Whole pounds only
Total value of purchases and all other inputs excluding any VAT. Include your Box 9 figure. (Box 7)	[ ] Whole pounds only
Total value of all supplies of goods and related costs, excluding any VAT, to other EC member states. (Box 8)	[ ] Whole pounds only
Total value of all acquisitions of goods and related costs, excluding any VAT, from other EC member states. (Box 9)	[ ] Whole pounds only

(b) **Calculate the values that will be shown online when you submit the VAT return for the following boxes. If a repayment is due, use a minus sign in Box 5.** **(4 marks)**

Total VAT due (the sum of boxes 1 and 2) (Box 3)

Net VAT to be paid to HM Revenue & Customs or reclaimed by you (difference between boxes 3 and 4) (Box 5)

Task 8 (10 marks)

You are an Accounting Technician for a business. It does not operate any special accounting schemes and has a direct debit arrangement in place with HMRC for VAT payments.

This is the completed online VAT return for the period ended 30 June.

Online VAT Return for period ended 30 June	
VAT due in this period on sales and other outputs. (Box 1)	87239.42
VAT due in this period on acquisitions from other EC member states. (Box 2)	0
Total VAT due (the sum of boxes 1 and 2). (Box 3)	**Calculated value**
VAT reclaimed in the period on purchases and other inputs (including acquisitions from the EC). (Box 4)	32987.13
Net VAT to be paid to HM Revenue & Customs or reclaimed by you (difference between boxes 3 and 4). (Box 5)	**Calculated value**
Total value of sales and all other outputs excluding any VAT. Include your Box 8 figure. (Box 6)	503976
Total value of purchases and other inputs excluding any VAT. Include your Box 9 figure. (Box 7)	164935
Total value of all supplies of goods and related costs, excluding any VAT, to other EC member states. (Box 8)	67779
Total value of all acquisitions of goods and related costs, excluding any VAT, from other EC member states. (Box 9)	0

Today's date is Thursday 16 July.

Bank working days are Monday to Friday. There are no bank holidays in July or the first half of August.

(a) **Complete the following email to the Finance Manager of the business.** **(8 marks)**

To:	Finance Manager
From:	Accounting Technician
Date:	Thursday 16 July
Subject:	Completed VAT return

Please be advised that I have just completed the online VAT return for the period ended 30 June.

The amount of VAT [▼] (1) will be [£ _____].

Please arrange

[_____ ▼] (2)

Kind regards,

Accounting Technician

The business is considering supplying a new service to business and non-business customers throughout the EU. The Sales Director wants a precise answer today about the exact rate of VAT to charge to all customers.

The Finance Manager is busy so instructs you to reply to the Sales Director. You are concerned that the detail required for the answer is beyond your current expertise.

Drop-down list:

(1) payable
    to be reclaimed

(2) to reclaim this amount in due course.

    to pay this electronically to arrive no later than Friday 31 July.

    to pay this electronically to arrive no later than Friday 7 August.

    for sufficient funds to permit HMRC to direct debit our account on Wednesday 12 August.

(b) **How should you respond to the Finance Manager's instruction?**

	✓
'OK, I think I know the answer so I will advise the Sales Director accordingly.'	
'I don't know the answer but I will advise the Sales Director that it is always best to charge VAT at 20%.'	
'I don't know the answer so I cannot advise the Sales Director without guidance from you.'	

AAT AQ2016 SAMPLE ASSESSMENT 1
INDIRECT TAX FA 2018

ANSWERS

Indirect Tax FA 2018 (IDRX)
AAT sample assessment 1

Task 1 (6 marks)

(a) **(i)** How much will the business have to pay HMRC in respect of output tax for its period of non-registration? The business has chosen to treat the amount charged as VAT-inclusive.

£	7,000

(ii) Must the business's customers reimburse the business for the output tax now payable to HMRC?

No

(b) Complete the following statement by choosing one option.

To find out information about registering on a special scheme for VAT, a business should, first of all, ...

	✓
... call HMRC on the General Enquiries helpline.	
... look at the HMRC website.	✓
... write to the HMRC.	

(c) Complete the following statement by choosing one option.

Voluntary registration for VAT is available to any business...

	✓
...with taxable turnover above the registration threshold.	
...that makes at least some taxable supplies.	✓

Task 2 (9 marks)

(a) Which one of the following amounts must appear on the simplified VAT invoice issued to the business?

£22	
£68	
£110	
£200	✓

(b) May the business issue a simplified invoice for this sale?

Yes	✓
No	

(c) Complete the following statement regarding the business's input tax for this period.

The business can reclaim | some | of its input tax because it makes | exempt supplies that are more than the *de minimus* amount.

(d) What is the tax point for this supply?

11 February.	✓
27 February.	

(e) What is the latest date by which it can issue a VAT invoice? Select one date from the calendar.

| 13 Aug |

Task 3 (5 marks)

(a) **Identify whether each of the following statements is true or false.**

	True	False
The due date for the VAT return is 31 October.		✓
Businesses that choose to pay VAT monthly must make at least nine VAT payments in any calendar year.	✓	

(b) **What is the earliest opportunity for the business to claim bad debt relief?**

	✓
In its VAT period ending 31 March.	
In its VAT period ending 30 June.	
In its VAT period ending 30 September.	✓
In its VAT period ending 31 December.	

Task 4 (9 marks)

(a) **Which correction should the business make in Box 1 of its current VAT return?**

	✓
Add £122.	
Add £234.	
Deduct £122.	
Deduct £234.	✓

(b) **Which of the following will be the consequence for the business?**

HMRC will regard this as...

	✓
... the correct action so there will be no further consequence.	
... the incorrect action and issue a surcharge liability notice.	
... a deliberate error and issue a penalty.	✓

(c) **Complete the following statement.**

A business's accountant needs to keep up-to-date with changes in VAT regulations and practice to comply with the ethical principle of

| professional competence. |

(d) **Identify whether each of the following statements about VAT rules and practice is true or false.**

	True	False
A business which fails to submit a VAT return may have to pay an amount which HMRC assesses to be due.	✓	
A business which receives a surcharge liability notice issued by HMRC must immediately pay a surcharge to HMRC.		✓

Task 5 (7 marks)

(a) **How much output tax should the business include in its VAT account for this supply?**

| £ | 148.20 |

(b) **How much output tax should the manufacturer include in its VAT account for this supply?**

| £ | 86.66 |

(c) **When the error is corrected, which one of the following figures will be correct?**

	✓
Input tax £1,313.	
Input tax £1,367.	✓
Output tax £5,463.	
Output tax £5,517.	

Task 6 (7 marks)

> **Rounding – (d) text box**
>
> These model answers show both rounded up and rounded down options. Both options are equally valid for the purposes of this assessment.

(a) **Which of the following should be your response to the business owner?**

	✓
If you insist then I will respect your authority and ignore the matter.	
Both VAT regulations and my ethical principles mean I cannot ignore the matter.	✓

(b) **Calculate the figure to be included in Box 1 of the VAT return, once any necessary corrections to the ledger accounts have been made.**

£ | 28,558.23

(c) **Calculate the figure to be included in Box 4 of the VAT return, once any necessary corrections to the ledger accounts have been made.**

£ | 14,572.81

(d) **Calculate the figure to be included in Box 6 of the VAT return, once any necessary corrections to the ledger accounts have been made. Your figure should be in whole pounds only.**

£ | 161,416 or 161,417

Task 7 (17 marks)

Rounding – (a) text boxes

These model answers show both rounded up and rounded down options. Both options are equally valid for the purposes of this assessment.

(a) **Enter the relevant figures into the online VAT return for the period ended 30 June. Do not leave any box blank.**

Online VAT Return for period ended 30 June	
Please note: Enter values in pounds sterling, including pence, for example 1000.00	
VAT due in this period on sales and other outputs. (Box 1)	55,673.82
VAT due in this period on acquisitions from other EC member states. (Box 2)	7,356.93
Total VAT due (the sum of boxes 1 and 2). (Box 3)	**Calculated value**
VAT reclaimed in the period on purchases and other inputs (including acquisitions from the EC). (Box 4)	20,351.87
Net VAT to be paid to HM Revenue & Customs or reclaimed by you (difference between boxes 3 and 4). (Box 5)	**Calculated value**
Total value of sales and all other outputs including any VAT. Include your Box 8 figure. (Box 6)	278,369 or 278,370 Whole pounds only
Total value of purchases and all other inputs excluding any VAT. Include your Box 9 figure. (Box 7)	101,759 or 101,760 Whole pounds only
Total value of all supplies of goods and related costs, excluding any VAT, to other EC member states. (Box 8)	0 Whole pounds only
Total value of all acquisitions of goods and related costs, excluding any VAT, from other EC member states. (Box 9)	36,784 or 36,785 Whole pounds only

(b) **Calculate the values that will be shown online when you submit the VAT return for the following boxes. If a repayment is due, use a minus sign in Box 5.**

Total VAT due (the sum of boxes 1 and 2) (Box 3) | 63,030.75 |

Net VAT to be paid to HM Revenue & Customs or reclaimed by you (difference between boxes 3 and 4) (Box 5) | 42,678.88 |

Task 8 (10 marks)

(a) **Complete the following email to the Finance Manager of the business.**

To:	Finance Manager
From:	Accounting Technician
Date:	Thursday 16 July
Subject:	Completed VAT return

Please be advised that I have just completed the online VAT return for the period ended 30 June.

The amount of VAT | payable | will be | £ | 54,252.29 |.

Please arrange

| for sufficient funds to permit HMRC to direct debit our account on Wednesday 12 August. |

Kind regards,

Accounting Technician

(b) **How should you respond to the Finance Manager's instruction?**

	✓
'OK, I think I know the answer so I will advise the Sales Director accordingly.'	
'I don't know the answer but I will advise the Sales Director that it is always best to charge VAT at 20%.'	
'I don't know the answer so I cannot advise the Sales Director without guidance from you.'	✓

AAT AQ2016 SAMPLE ASSESSMENT 2 INDIRECT TAX FA 2018

You are advised to attempt sample assessment 2 online from the AAT website. This will ensure you are prepared for how the assessment will be presented on the AAT's system when you attempt the real assessment. Please access the assessment using the address below:

https://www.aat.org.uk/training/study-support/search

The AAT may call the assessments on their website, under study support resources, either a 'practice assessment' or 'sample assessment'.

BPP PRACTICE ASSESSMENT 1
INDIRECT TAX FA 2018

Time allowed: 1 hour and 30 minutes

Indirect Tax (IDRX)
BPP practice assessment 1

Task 1

Joseph makes zero-rated supplies and Julie makes standard-rated supplies. Both are considering voluntarily registering for VAT. Julie's customers are mostly VAT-registered themselves.

(a)   Identify whether the following statements are true or false.

TICK ONE BOX per statement.

	True	False
Joseph will be in a repayment position if he voluntarily registers.		
Julie's customers will not suffer the impact of her charging VAT unless they are not VAT-registered.		

Clover Ltd has been trading for 12 months. You have extracted the following information in relation to the company.

Turnover	VAT excl £
Standard-rated	60,000
Zero-rated	18,000
Exempt	8,000

(b)   Identify whether the following statement is true or false.

TICK ONE BOX

(Assuming Clover Ltd was not VAT-registered from starting to trade)

	True	False
Clover Ltd must VAT register as total turnover exceeds £85,000.		

(c)   Complete the following statement by choosing one option.

To find out information about VAT on overseas supplies, the **final** action a taxpayer should take is to:

	✓
...call HMRC on the General Enquiries helpline.	
...look at the HMRC website.	
....write to the HMRC.	

Task 2

Adam is a VAT-registered trader making standard-rated supplies. On 19 March 20X0 he received an order from a customer together with a 10% deposit including VAT of £40. The goods were sent out to the customer on 22 March 20X0. An invoice was sent out on 1 April 20X0 that included VAT of £400. The customer paid the balance of the invoice (including VAT of £360) on 30 April 20X0.

Calculate the amount of output tax to be included on Adam's VAT return to:

(a) **31 March 20X0**

TICK ONE BOX

	✓
Nil	
£40	
£360	
£400	

(b) **30 June 20X0**

TICK ONE BOX

	✓
Nil	
£40	
£360	
£400	

A VAT-registered business makes a mixture of exempt and taxable supplies.

(c) **Which of the following statements is/are true?** TICK ONE BOX

	✓
Only the input tax relating to taxable supplies is recoverable, in all circumstances.	
All input tax is recoverable if certain *de minimis* tests are satisfied.	
No input tax is recoverable.	
All input tax is recoverable as no supplies are outside the scope of VAT.	

Task 3

Igor has been trading for many years and makes standard-rated supplies. He is in the flat rate scheme. The flat rate percentage that he must use is 10.5%.

In the latest quarter, Igor had total turnover of £9,000 excluding VAT. He also had VAT-exclusive purchases of £2,000.

(a) **Identify which one of the following is the output tax figure to be included in Igor's VAT return.**

TICK ONE BOX

	✓
£945.00	
£1,134.00	
£882.00	

(b) **In this quarter, would Igor have more or less VAT to pay to HMRC if he was not in the flat rate scheme?**

TICK ONE BOX

	✓
More VAT payable if not in the flat rate scheme	
Less VAT payable if not in the flat rate scheme	

(c) **Which one of the following is not a valid reason for a business making taxable supplies choosing to operate the annual accounting scheme?**

TICK ONE BOX

	✓
Only one VAT return per annum is required.	
It helps regulate cash flow.	
It reduces the administrative burden on the business.	
Only one VAT payment per annum is required.	

Task 4

You have extracted the following information from the accounting records of a VAT-registered client.

Detail	Net £	VAT £	Gross £
Car (for use by salesman)	14,000.00	2,800.00	16,800.00
Hotels (for sales reps while on business)	2,400.00	480.00	2,880.00
UK client lunches	460.00	92.00	552.00

(a) **Calculate the total amount of input tax that is recoverable by the client relating to these items of expenditure.**

TICK ONE BOX

	✓
Nil	
£92.00	
£480.00	
£3,372.00	

(b) **Identify whether the following statements are true or false.**

TICK ONE BOX PER STATEMENT.

	True	False
If a trader submits an inaccurate VAT return but tells HMRC of the inaccuracy as soon as possible, this may reduce the possible penalty.		
Tax evasion is illegal and may lead to fines and imprisonment.		

A business has turnover of £2,000,000 and has discovered an error in its last VAT return that has resulted in an underpayment of £12,500.

(c) **What is the correct action to take?**

TICK ONE BOX

	✓
Ignore the error	
Correct the error on the next VAT return	
Disclose the error separately through a Form 652	

Task 5

A trader sells goods with a list price of £200 plus VAT at the standard rate but offers a settlement discount of 5% for payment within 30 days. The customer pays after 45 days. The trader's original invoice was for the discounted amount.

(a) What action does the trader now need to take?

TICK ONE BOX

	✓
Re-issue an invoice for the full price	
Issue an invoice for the amount of the discount	
No action is required	
Issue a credit note for the discount	

The correct VAT payable by a business for the quarter ended 31 December 20X1 is shown on the VAT return as £18,400.00. However, the VAT account at the end of this period shows a balance of £28,400.00.

(b) Which of the following statements could explain the difference?

TICK ONE BOX

	✓
The VAT payment for the previous period of £5,000.00 was not posted to the VAT account.	
The VAT payment for the previous period of £5,000.00 was posted to the wrong side of the VAT account.	

A manufacturer supplies a reduced-rate item at a VAT inclusive price of £1,575.

(c) How much output tax should the manufacturer include in its VAT account for this supply?

£ [ ]

Task 6

The following accounts have been extracted from Company A's ledgers for quarter ended 31 December 20X0.

Sales day book summary

	Zero-rated sales £	Standard-rated sales £	VAT £	Total £
UK sales	15,000.00	70,000.00	14,000.00	99,000.00

Purchases day book summary

	Zero-rated purchases £	Standard-rated purchases £	VAT £	Total £
UK purchases/expenses	2,500.00	17,200.00	3,440.00	23,140.00

Purchases returns day book summary

	Standard-rated purchases £	VAT £	Total £
UK purchases	2,300.00	460.00	2,760.00

In December 20X0 two debts (on standard-rated sales) were written off as irrecoverable (bad) in Company A's accounting records. The first debt was for £758 on an invoice dated 15 March 20X0; the second was for £622 with an invoice dated 23 June 20X0. Company A's payment terms are strictly 30 days from date of invoice. Both figures are stated inclusive of VAT.

(a) **Calculate the figure to be reclaimed for bad debt relief in the quarter ended 31/12/X0.**

The figure to be reclaimed for bad debt relief is:	£	

(b) **Calculate the figure for Box 1 of the VAT return quarter ended 31/12/X0.**

The figure for Box 1 of the VAT return is:	£	

(c) **Calculate the figure for Box 4 of the VAT return quarter ended 31/12/X0.**

The figure for Box 4 of the VAT return is:	£	

The owner of the business is putting pressure on you to claim bad debt relief that is not due yet.

(d) How should you respond?

	✓
I work for the owner and therefore will follow his instructions.	
To carry out his instructions would breach the principle of confidentiality, so I should refuse.	
To carry out his instructions would breach the principle of integrity, so I should refuse.	

Task 7

This task is about completing a VAT return for Company B.

The following details have been extracted from the company's accounting ledgers:

QUARTER ENDED 31 MARCH 20X0

Sales account

Date	Reference	Debit £	Date	Reference	Credit £
			01/01/X0–31/03/X0	Sales day book -UK sales	797,830.00
31/03/X0	Balance c/d	872,990.00	01/01/X0–31/03/X0	Sales day book -Zero-rated EU despatches	75,160.00
	Total	872,990.00		Total	872,990.00

Purchases/expenses account

Date	Reference	Debit £	Date	Reference	Credit £
31/03/X0	Purchases day book	520,565.00	01/01/X0–31/03/X0	Balance c/d	520,565.00
	Total	520,565.00		Total	520,565.00

VAT account

Date	Reference	Debit £	Date	Reference	Credit £
01/01/X0 –31/03/X0	Purchases day book	104,113.00	01/01/X0– 31/03/X0	Sales day book	159,566.00

A debt of £606.00, inclusive of VAT, was written-off as irrecoverable (bad) in March 20X0. The related sale was due for payment ten months ago. Bad debt relief is now to be claimed.

Complete Boxes 1 to 9 of the VAT return below for quarter ended 31 March 20X0.

VAT return for quarter ended 31 March 20X0		£
VAT due in this period on **sales** and other outputs	Box 1	
VAT due in this period on **acquisitions** from other **EC Member States**	Box 2	
Total VAT due **(the sum of Boxes 1 and 2)**	Box 3	
VAT reclaimed in the period on **purchases** and other inputs, including acquisitions from the EC	Box 4	
Net VAT to be paid to HM Revenue & Customs or reclaimed by you **(difference between Boxes 3 and 4)**	Box 5	
Total value of **sales** and all other outputs excluding any VAT. **Include your Box 8 figure**	Box 6	
Total value of purchases and all other inputs excluding any VAT. **Include your Box 9 figure**	Box 7	
Total value of all **supplies** of goods and related costs, excluding any VAT, to other **EC Member States**	Box 8	
Total value of all **acquisitions** of goods and related costs, excluding any VAT, from other **EC Member States**	Box 9	

Task 8

You work in a large company, and have just completed the VAT return for the quarter ended 31 March 20X1. The VAT return showed an amount of £8,000.00 in Box 1 and in Box 3, and an amount of £2,000.00 in Box 4.

(a) **Complete the memo to the financial controller regarding the payment of VAT for this quarter.**

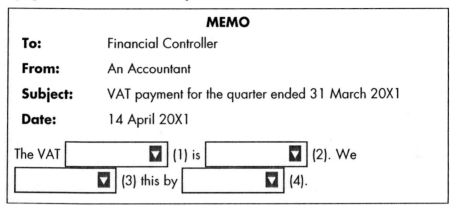

MEMO	
To:	Financial Controller
From:	An Accountant
Subject:	VAT payment for the quarter ended 31 March 20X1
Date:	14 April 20X1

The VAT [▼] (1) is [▼] (2). We [▼] (3) this by [▼] (4).

Picklist:

(1) payable
   repayable

(2) £8,000.00
   £2,000.00
   £6,000.00

(3) must pay
   will receive

(4) 30 April 20X1
   7 May 20X1

You have discovered that your predecessor has destroyed the VAT invoices relating to two accounting periods.

(b) **What is the maximum penalty that may apply?**

TICK ONE BOX

	✓
£0	
£3,000	
£6,000	
£24,000	

BPP PRACTICE ASSESSMENT 1
INDIRECT TAX FA 2018

ANSWERS

Indirect Tax
BPP practice assessment 1

Task 1

(a)

	True	False
Joseph will be in a repayment position if he voluntarily registers.	✓	
Julie's customers will not suffer the impact of her charging VAT unless they are not VAT-registered.	✓	

(b)

	True	False
Clover Ltd must VAT-register as total turnover exceeds £85,000.		✓

Only taxable turnover is considered when determining whether the threshold has been exceeded. Taxable turnover is £78,000.

(c)

	✓
...call HMRC on the General Enquiries helpline.	
...look at the HMRC website.	
....write to the HMRC.	✓

....

Task 2

(a)   31 March 20X0

	✓
Nil	
£40	✓
£360	
£400	

(b)   30 June 20X0

	✓
Nil	
£40	
£360	✓
£400	

(c)

	✓
Only the input tax relating to taxable supplies is recoverable, in all circumstances.	
All input tax is recoverable if certain *de minimis* tests are satisfied.	✓
No input tax is recoverable.	
All input tax is recoverable as no supplies are outside the scope of VAT.	

Task 3

(a)

	✓
£945.00	
£1,134.00	✓
£882.00	

(£9,000 × 120%) × 10.5% = £1,134.00

(b)

	✓
More VAT payable if not in the flat rate scheme	✓
Less VAT payable if not in the flat rate scheme	

If not in the flat rate scheme Igor's VAT payable would be:

		£
Output tax	£9,000 × 20%	1,800.00
Input tax	£2,000 × 20%	(400.00)
		1,400.00

As this is more than £1,134.00 Igor would have more VAT payable.

(c)

	✓
Only one VAT return per annum is required.	
It helps regulate cash flow.	
It reduces the administrative burden on the business.	
Only one VAT payment per annum is required.	✓

Task 4

(a)

	✓
Nil	
£92.00	
£480.00	✓
£3,372.00	

VAT is irrecoverable on cars with an element of private use and on business entertaining.

(b)

	True	False
If a trader submits an inaccurate VAT return but tells HMRC of the inaccuracy as soon as possible, this may reduce the possible penalty.	✓	
Tax evasion is illegal and may lead to fines and imprisonment.	✓	

(c)

	✓
Ignore the error	
Correct the error on the next VAT return	✓
Disclose the error separately through a Form 652	

The error is less than the higher of £10,000 or 1% of turnover (£20,000), and can therefore be corrected by adjusting the next VAT return.

Task 5

(a)

	✓
Re-issue an invoice for the full price	
Issue an invoice for the amount of the discount (not taken up by customer)	✓
No action is required	
Issue a credit note for the discount	

(b)

	✓
The VAT payment for the previous period of £5,000.00 was not posted to the VAT account.	
The VAT payment for the previous period of £5,000.00 was posted to the wrong side of the VAT account.	✓

(c)

£	75.00

£1,575 × 5/105

....

Task 6

(a)

The figure to be reclaimed for bad debt relief is:	£	126.33

£758 × 1/6 = £126.33

(b)

The figure for Box 1 of the VAT return is:	£	14,000.00

(c)

The figure for Box 4 of the VAT return is:	£	3,106.33

£3,440.00 − £460.00 + £126.33

(d)

	✓
I work for the owner and therefore will follow his instructions.	
To carry out his instructions would breach the principle of confidentiality, so I should refuse.	
To carry out his instructions would breach the principle of integrity, so I should refuse.	✓

Task 7

VAT return for quarter ended 31 March 20X0		£
VAT due in this period on **sales** and other outputs	**Box 1**	159,566.00
VAT due in this period on **acquisitions** from other **EC Member States**	**Box 2**	0
Total VAT due **(the sum of Boxes 1 and 2)**	**Box 3**	159,566.00
VAT reclaimed in the period on **purchases** and other inputs, including acquisitions from the EC	**Box 4**	104,214.00
Net VAT to be paid to HM Revenue & Customs or reclaimed by you **(difference between Boxes 3 and 4)**	**Box 5**	55,352.00
Total value of **sales** and all other outputs excluding any VAT. **Include your Box 8 figure**	**Box 6**	872,990
Total value of purchases and all other inputs excluding any VAT. **Include your Box 9 figure**	**Box 7**	520,565
Total value of all **supplies** of goods and related costs, excluding any VAT, to other **EC Member States**	**Box 8**	75,160
Total value of all **acquisitions** of goods and related costs, excluding any VAT, from other **EC Member States**	**Box 9**	0

Workings: Box 4 = £104,113.00 + (£606.00 × 1/6) = £104,214.00

Task 8

(a)

MEMO

To: Financial Controller

From: An Accountant

Subject: VAT payment for the quarter ended 31 March 20X1

Date: 14 April 20X1

The VAT [**payable**] is [**£6,000.00**]. We [**must pay**] this by [**7 May 20X1.**]

(b)

	✓
£0	
£3,000	
£6,000	✓
£24,000	

BPP PRACTICE ASSESSMENT 2
INDIRECT TAX FA 2018

Time allowed: 1 hour and 30 minutes

Indirect Tax (IDRX)
BPP practice assessment 2

Task 1

A trader wants to know whether a new type of supply he is making is a taxable supply. He has consulted the HMRC website and cannot resolve his query.

(a) What should be his next course of action?

TICK ONE BOX

	✓
Email his HMRC contact	
Write a letter to HMRC	
Telephone the VAT enquiries number	

During the first nine months of trade, a business made zero-rated supplies totalling £41,000 and exempt supplies totalling £45,000.

(b) Which of the following statements is TRUE?

TICK ONE BOX

	✓
The trader must register for VAT as his supplies have exceeded the VAT registration threshold.	
The trader cannot register for VAT as he does not make any standard-rated supplies.	
The trader was automatically registered for VAT as soon as he started trading.	
The trader can voluntarily register for VAT as he makes some taxable supplies.	

John, a trader, failed to register for VAT on time, and standard-rated sales invoiced since registration became effective have totalled £75,000. John has approached the customers but they have refused to pay the VAT.

(c) What amount of VAT will John have to pay to HMRC?

£ [ ]

....

Task 2

(a) Identify whether the following statement is true or false.

TICK ONE BOX

	True	False
The basic tax point for goods is when an order is received.		

(b) Identify whether the following statements in relation to VAT invoices are true or false.

TICK ONE BOX

	True	False
A VAT invoice must include certain details including the supplier's VAT registration number, the total VAT payable and a description of the goods supplied.		
A less detailed invoice may be issued if the VAT inclusive proceeds are less than £150.		
If a sale is made to a VAT-registered customer in the EU, the invoice must include the standard rate of VAT unless the invoice includes the customer's VAT number.		

(c) Which of the following statements is TRUE about a VAT-registered company making both standard-rated and exempt supplies?

TICK ONE BOX

	✓
No input VAT can be recovered.	
All input VAT can always be recovered because the company makes some taxable supplies.	
All input VAT can be recovered, provided certain de minimis limits are not exceeded.	

Task 3

Gomez uses the annual accounting scheme for his business. The business's VAT liability for the year ended 30 June 20X0 was £15,000 and for the following year, the year ended 30 June 20X1 was £18,500.

(a)   The final balancing payment for the year ended 30 June X1 is:

TICK ONE BOX

	✓
£Nil	
£3,500	
£5,000	
£18,500	

(b)   The final balancing payment is due by:

TICK ONE BOX

	✓
30 June 20X1	
30 July 20X1	
31 July 20X1	
31 August 20X1	

Xavier has a quarter ended 31 December 20X0. His normal payment terms are one calendar month after invoice date.

(c)   Identify whether bad debt relief can be claimed in respect of the following amounts owed to Xavier as at 31 December 20X0.

Moraira Ltd owes £3,000 from an invoice issued on 2 January 20X0. Xavier believes that the amount will be paid in full and so it has not been written-off in the accounts.

TICK ONE BOX

	✓
Bad debt relief can be claimed.	
Bad debt relief cannot be claimed.	

Calpe Ltd owes £2,000 from an invoice issued on 15 June 20X0. Xavier does not expect that the amount will be paid and so it has been written-off in the accounts.

TICK ONE BOX

	✓
Bad debt relief can be claimed.	
Bad debt relief cannot be claimed.	

Task 4

(a) Failing to register for VAT at the right time may lead to:

TICK ONE BOX

	✓
A surcharge liability notice	
A surcharge	
A penalty	
No consequences	

Claudia deliberately understated her output VAT on her last return but now she wishes to correct this.

(b) Identify which one of the following statements is the correct action Claudia must take to correct the error.

TICK ONE BOX

	✓
The error can be adjusted for on the next return, but Claudia must also inform HMRC separately and she may be liable to a penalty.	
The error cannot be adjusted on the next return, so Claudia must inform HMRC separately in writing, and will not be liable to a penalty.	
The error cannot be adjusted on the next return, so Claudia must inform HMRC separately in writing, and may also be liable to a penalty.	

(c) Identify whether the following statement is true or false.

TICK ONE BOX

	True	False
The VAT fuel scale charge is the amount of input tax recoverable on private fuel purchases.		

(d) **Complete the following sentence.**

The disclosure to HMRC of a VAT error, in the absence of consent from the client, is a breach of the fundamental principle of [▼   ]

Picklist:

confidentiality.
integrity.
professional competence and due care.

Task 5

(a) **Insert the missing VAT figures in the unshaded boxes of the table below.**

Net £	VAT @ 20% £	Gross £
		270.60
260.00		

A business has completed its VAT return, which shows a correct amount of £5,600.00 owing to HMRC. The VAT account at the end of the same period shows a liability of £8,000.00.

(b) **Which of the following could explain this difference?**

TICK ONE BOX.

	✓
The VAT payment for the previous period of £2,400 has not been entered in the VAT account.	
The VAT payment for the previous period of £2,400 has been entered twice in the VAT account.	

Task 6

This task is about preparing figures for a VAT Return for a business run by Joseph Marselus for the period ended 31 March 20X0.

Sales are made at the standard rate.

The following accounts have been extracted from Joseph's ledgers.

Sales and sales returns account

Date 20X0	Reference	Debit £	Date 20X0	Reference	Credit £
01/01–31/03	Sales returns day book - UK sales returns	13,000.00	01/01–31/03	Sales day book - UK sales	275,000.00
31/03	Balance c/d	262,000.00			
	Total	275,000.00		Total	275,000.00

Purchases account

Date 20X0	Reference	Debit £	Date 20X0	Reference	Credit £
01/01–31/03	Purchases day book - UK purchases	101,000.00	31/03	Balance c/d	101,000.00
	Total	101,000.00		Total	101,000.00

VAT account

Date 20X0	Reference	Debit £	Date 20X0	Reference	Credit £
01/01–31/03	Sales returns day book	2,600.00	01/01–31/03	Sales day book	55,000.00
01/01–31/03	Purchases day book	20,200.00			

Joseph Marselus accidentally left out a couple of invoices from his last VAT return.

- Invoice 1 was for £3,400.00 (VAT-exclusive) to a customer
- Invoice 2 was for £254.00 (VAT-exclusive) from a supplier

He is able to correct them on his next return.

(a) **Calculate the net VAT adjustment figure needed to correct these errors.**

£ [   ]

Joseph wants to correct only Invoice 2.

(b) **Are the following statements true or false?**

	True	False
I should follow Joseph's instructions as he is the business owner.		
I should disclose both errors to HMRC without Joseph's consent.		
I should make Joseph aware that deliberate underpayment of VAT is tax evasion which is a crime.		

(c) **Calculate the figure for Box 1 of the VAT Return.**

£ [   ]

(d) **Calculate the figure for Box 4 of the VAT Return.**

£ [   ]

Task 7

This task is about completing a VAT return for Gilbert Jones Ltd.

The following details have been extracted from the company's accounting records for the period August to October 20X0.

Sales: UK – standard-rated

Date		Dr £	Cr £
31/08/X0	Sales day book		185,463.00
30/09/X0	Sales day book		186,795.00
31/10/X0	Sales day book		189,674.00
TOTAL			**561,932.00**

Sales: EU despatches – zero-rated

Date		Dr £	Cr £
31/08/X0	Sales day book		10,856.00
30/09/X0	Sales day book		9,745.00
31/10/X0	Sales day book		8,796.00
TOTAL			**29,397.00**

Purchases: UK – standard-rate

Date		Dr £	Cr £
31/08/X0	Purchases day book	62,758.00	
30/09/X0	Purchases day book	64,241.00	
31/10/X0	Purchases day book	65,913.00	
TOTAL		**192,912.00**	

Purchases: EU acquisitions – standard-rated

Date		Dr £	Cr £
31/08/X0	Purchases day book	0	
30/09/X0	Purchases day book	0	
31/10/X0	Purchases day book	15,400.00	
TOTAL		**15,400.00**	

VAT: Output tax

Date		Dr £	Cr £
31/08/X0	Sales day book		37,092.60
30/09/X0	Sales day book		37,359.00
31/10/X0	Sales day book		37,934.80
TOTAL			**112,386.40**

VAT: Input tax

Date		Dr £	Cr £
31/08/X0	Purchases day book	12,551.60	
30/09/X0	Purchases day book	12,848.20	
31/10/X0	Purchases day book	16,262.60	
TOTAL		**41,662.40**	

(a) **Complete Boxes 1 to 9 of the VAT return below for quarter ended 31 October 20X0**

VAT return for quarter ended 31 October 20X0		£
Please note: insert values in pounds sterling, including pence, for example 1000.00		
VAT due in this period on **sales** and other outputs	**Box 1**	
VAT due in this period on **acquisitions** from other **EC Member States**	**Box 2**	
Total VAT due **(the sum of Boxes 1 and 2)**	**Box 3**	Calculated value
VAT reclaimed in the period on **purchases** and other inputs, including acquisitions from the EC	**Box 4**	
Net VAT to be paid to HM Revenue & Customs or reclaimed by you **(difference between Boxes 3 and 4)**	**Box 5**	Calculated value
Total value of **sales** and all other outputs excluding any VAT. **Include your Box 8 figure**	**Box 6**	
Total value of purchases and all other inputs excluding any VAT. **Include your Box 9 figure**	**Box 7**	
Total value of all **supplies** of goods and related costs, excluding any VAT, to other **EC Member States**	**Box 8**	
Total value of all **acquisitions** of goods and related costs, excluding any VAT, from other **EC Member States**	**Box 9**	

(b) **Calculate the values for Box 3 and Box 5 that will be shown online when you submit the VAT return. If a repayment is due, use a minus sign in Box 5.**

Total VAT due **(the sum of Boxes 1 and 2)** (Box 3) [ ]

Net VAT to be paid to HM Revenue & Customs or reclaimed by you **(difference between Boxes 3 and 4)** (Box 5) [ ]

Task 8

You work for a firm of accountants. One of your clients Donald Smith Ltd has provided you with the following information. It is 12 Nov 20X0.

The Showroom of Donald Smith Ltd sold some goods for £15,000 plus VAT to a customer, GHA Stores plc, in February 20X0 on 30 days' credit. Donald Smith Ltd was informed yesterday that GHA Stores plc had ceased trading and the debt is irrecoverable. This is the first time that Donald Smith Ltd has had a substantial bad debt. Donald Smith Ltd has a VAT registration number of 482 912 5407.

You are required to write to Donald Smith Ltd, explaining the steps that Donald Smith Ltd needs to take in order to claim bad debt relief for the VAT element of this debt, and the timescale in which the steps should be taken so that relief is obtained as soon as possible. Donald's next VAT return will be for the quarter ending 31 January 20X1.

ABC Accountants

Tate House, Henry Road, Guildford, Surrey. GU8 5CM

Telephone: 01344 627896

Donald Smith Ltd
Park Drive Trading Estate
Sunninghill Road
Ascot
Berks
BU8 5ZD

12 November 20X0

Dear Sirs

I understand you have recently been informed that a net sale of £ [_____] ▼ (1) to GHA Stores plc in February on 30 days' credit is now a bad debt.

The steps set out below will enable you to claim bad debt relief for the VAT element of the debt (£ [_____] ▼ (2)) in your next VAT return.

*   Write off the entire debt of £ [_____] ▼ (1) in your accounts before 31 January 20X1

*   Retain a copy of the VAT invoice and the journal writing it off

*   In your next VAT return, for the quarter ending 31 January 20X1 (when the debt will be more than [_____] ▼ (3) months overdue), add £ [_____] ▼ (2) to Box [____] ▼ (4) (input tax box).

If you have any further queries please do not hesitate to contact me.

Yours faithfully

Deputy Accountant

Picklist:

(1):
18,000
21,600
15,000

(2):
3,000.00
3,600.00

(3):
6
12

(4):
1
4

....

BPP PRACTICE ASSESSMENT 2
INDIRECT TAX FA 2018

ANSWERS

Indirect Tax (IDRX)
BPP practice assessment 2

Task 1

(a)

	✓
Email his HMRC contact	
Write a letter to HMRC	
Telephone the VAT enquiries number	✓

(b)

	✓
The trader must register for VAT as his supplies have exceeded the VAT registration threshold.	
The trader cannot register for VAT as he does not make any standard-rated supplies.	
The trader was automatically registered for VAT as soon as he started trading.	
The trader can voluntarily register for VAT as he makes some taxable supplies.	✓

(c)

£	12,500

Sales are deemed to be VAT inclusive. £75,000 × 20/120 = £12,500

....

Task 2

(a)

	True	False
The basic tax point for goods is when they are made available.		✓

Receipt of an order is never a tax point.

(b)

	True	False
A VAT invoice must include certain details including the supplier's VAT registration number, the total VAT payable and a description of the goods supplied.	✓	
A less detailed invoice may be issued if the VAT-inclusive proceeds are less than £150.		✓
If a sale is made to a VAT-registered customer in the EU, the invoice must include the standard rate of VAT unless the invoice includes the customer's VAT number.	✓	

(c)

	✓
No input VAT can be recovered.	
All input VAT can always be recovered because the company makes some taxable supplies.	
All input VAT can be recovered, provided certain de minimis limits are not exceeded.	✓

Task 3

(a)

	✓
£Nil	
£3,500	
£5,000	✓
£18,500	

£18,500 − (£15,000 × 90%)

(b)

	✓
30 June 20X1	
30 July 20X1	
31 July 20X1	
31 August 20X1	✓

Within 2 months of VAT annual period.

(c) Moraira Ltd

	✓
Bad debt relief can be claimed.	
Bad debt relief cannot be claimed.	✓

The debt has not been written off in the accounts

Calpe Ltd

	✓
Bad debt relief can be claimed.	
Bad debt relief cannot be claimed.	✓

It is less than six months since the debt was due for payment (15 July 20X0).

Task 4

(a)

	✓
A surcharge liability notice	
A surcharge	
A penalty	✓
No consequences	

(b)

	✓
The error can be adjusted for on the next return, but Claudia must also inform HMRC separately and she may be liable to a penalty.	
The error cannot be adjusted on the next return, so Claudia must inform HMRC separately in writing, and will not be liable to a penalty.	
The error cannot be adjusted on the next return, so Claudia must inform HMRC separately in writing, and may also be liable to a penalty.	✓

(c)

	True	False
The VAT fuel scale charge is the amount of input tax recoverable on private fuel purchases.		✓

The fuel scale charge is an amount of output tax to offset against the input tax reclaimed on fuel purchase invoices.

(d) The disclosure to HMRC of a VAT error, in the absence of consent from the client, is a breach of the fundamental principle of **confidentiality**

Task 5

(a)

Net £	VAT @ 20% £	Gross £
	45.10	270.60
260.00	52.00	

£270.60 × 1/6 = £45.10

£260.00 × 20% = £52.00

(b)

	✓
The VAT payment for the previous period of £2,400 has not been entered in the VAT account.	✓
The VAT payment for the previous period of £2,400 has been entered twice in the VAT account.	

If the payment for the previous period had been posted in the VAT account, the liability showing would be £8,000.00 – £2,400.00 = £5,600.00 ie the liability for the current period.

If the previous payment had been entered twice, the balance showing on the VAT account would have been too low by £2,400.00 ie would have been £3,200.00.

Task 6

(a)

£ | 629.20

($3,400 × 20%$) – ($254 × 20%$)

(b)

	True	False
I should follow Joseph's instructions as he is the business owner.		✓
I should disclose both errors to HMRC without Joseph's consent.		✓
I should make Joseph aware that deliberate underpayment of VAT is tax evasion which is a crime.	✓	

(c) **Box 1 of the VAT Return.**

£ | 53,029.20

£55,000.00 – £2,600.00 + net error £629.20

If there is more than one error, they are netted off, and one adjustment is made. Here there is a net understatement of output tax and so the figure in Box 1 is increased.

(d) **Box 4 of the VAT Return.**

£ | 20,200.00

Task 7

(a)

VAT return for quarter ended 31 October 20X0		£
VAT due in this period on **sales** and other outputs	**Box 1**	112,386.40
VAT due in this period on **acquisitions** from other **EC Member States**	**Box 2**	3,080.00
Total VAT due **(the sum of Boxes 1 and 2)**	**Box 3**	Calculated value
VAT reclaimed in the period on **purchases** and other inputs, including acquisitions from the EC	**Box 4**	44,742.40
Net VAT to be paid to HM Revenue & Customs or reclaimed by you **(difference between Boxes 3 and 4)**	**Box 5**	Calculated value
Total value of **sales** and all other outputs excluding any VAT. **Include your Box 8 figure**	**Box 6**	591,329
Total value of purchases and all other inputs excluding any VAT. **Include your Box 9 figure**	**Box 7**	208,312
Total value of all **supplies** of goods and related costs, excluding any VAT, to other **EC Member States**	**Box 8**	29,397
Total value of all **acquisitions** of goods and related costs, excluding any VAT, from other **EC Member States**	**Box 9**	15,400

Workings:

		£
Box 4	VAT on UK purchases	41,662.40
	VAT on EU acquisitions	3,080.00
		44,742.40

		£
Box 6	UK sales	561,932.00
	EU sales	29,397.00
		591,329.00

	£
Box 7	Purchases day book	192,912.00
	Purchases	
	EU acquisitions	15,400.00
		208,312.00

(b) Box 3 £115,466.40

Box 5 £70,724.00

··

Task 8

ABC Accountants

Tate House, Henry Road, Guildford, Surrey. GU8 5CM
Telephone 01344 627896

Donald Smith Ltd
Park Drive Trading Estate
Sunninghill Road
Ascot
Berks
BU8 5ZD

12 November 20X0

Dear Sirs

I understand you have recently been informed that a net sale of **£15,000** to GHA Stores plc in February on 30 days' credit is now a bad debt.

The steps set out below will enable you to claim bad debt relief for the VAT element of the debt **(£3,000.00)** in your next VAT return.

- Write off the entire debt of **£18,000** in your accounts before 31 January 20X1

- Retain a copy of the VAT invoice and the journal writing it off

- In your next VAT return, for the quarter ending 31 January 20X1 (when the debt will be more than **6** months overdue), add **£3,000.00** to Box **4** (input tax box).

If you have any further queries please do not hesitate to contact me.

Yours faithfully

Deputy Accountant

BPP PRACTICE ASSESSMENT 3
INDIRECT TAX FA 2018

Time allowed: 1 hour and 30 minutes

This practice assessment is presented in the format for the AQ2013 assessment. However the content of this practice assessment will be valid for students sitting under AQ2016.

PRACTICE ASSESSMENT 3

Indirect Tax (IDRX)
BPP practice assessment 3

Task 1

It is 31 December, Julian has been trading for ten months and his taxable turnover has consistently been £7,500 per month. Next month's turnover is expected to be the same.

(a) Indicate whether Julian should register for VAT immediately or monitor his turnover and register later.

TICK ONE BOX

	✓
Register immediately	
Monitor turnover and register later	

It is 31 December, Jasper has been trading for ten months and his taxable turnover has consistently been £6,500 per month. Next month he is expecting additional payment of £80,000, in addition to his normal monthly turnover.

(b) Indicate whether Julian should register for VAT immediately or monitor his turnover and register later.

TICK ONE BOX

	✓
Register immediately	
Monitor turnover and register later	

Task 2

(a) Identify whether the statement below is true or false.

TICK ONE BOX

	True	False
A business makes supplies that are both standard-rated and zero-rated. All of the input VAT can be reclaimed providing certain (*de minimis*) conditions are met.		

A registered trader receives an order for goods on 15 June 20X1. The trader delivers the goods to the customer on 20 June 20X1, and issues an invoice on 23 June 20X1. The customer pays for the goods in full on 2 July 20X1.

(b) Identify the tax point for this transaction.

TICK ONE BOX

15 June 20X1	
20 June 20X1	
23 June 20X1	
2 July 20X1	

(c) Identify with a tick which TWO of the following do not need to be included on a valid VAT invoice.

	✓
VAT number of supplier	
Invoice date	
VAT number of customer	
Rate of VAT	
Total price excluding VAT for each type of item	
Total amount of VAT for each type of item	
Total price including VAT for each type of item	
Name and address of customer	
Name and address of supplier	

Task 3

A business operates the cash accounting scheme.

(a) Indicate which one of the following statements would be a benefit of using this scheme.

TICK ONE BOX

	✓
Only having to submit one VAT return a year	
Automatic bad debt relief	
Paying a percentage of turnover over to HMRC	

A business operates the annual accounting scheme.

(b) **Indicate which one of the following statements would be correct when using this scheme.**

TICK ONE BOX

	✓
Each year, the business submits one annual return and makes one payment.	
Each year, the business submits one annual return and makes ten payments.	
Each year, the business submits one annual return and makes four payments.	

A business operates the flat rate scheme.

(c) **Indicate which one of the following statements would be correct when using this scheme.**

TICK ONE BOX

	✓
The business pays a percentage of tax-inclusive turnover to HMRC and reclaims input VAT.	
The business pays a percentage of tax-exclusive turnover to HMRC and reclaims input VAT.	
The business pays a percentage of tax-inclusive turnover to HMRC and cannot reclaim input VAT.	
The business pays a percentage of tax-exclusive turnover to HMRC and cannot reclaim input VAT.	

Task 4

Vince is an employee of Brown Ltd and he has the use of a company car which he uses both privately and for business. Brown Ltd pays for all the petrol costs on the car for the quarter, and recovers all the input tax on these costs.

(a) **Which of the following statements is TRUE?**

TICK ONE BOX

	✓
Brown Ltd must charge an amount of output tax (the fuel scale charge) to reflect the private use.	
Brown Ltd must charge an amount of input tax (the fuel scale charge) to reflect the private use.	

Victoria made an error on her last VAT return. She needs to inform HMRC in writing preferably by completing form 652 'Notification of Errors in VAT Returns'.

(b) **Identify with a tick any of the following statements that could be correct in relation to this error.**

	✓
The error is less than the error correction reporting threshold, but deliberate.	
The error is less than the error correction reporting threshold, but not deliberate.	
The error is more than the error correction reporting threshold, and deliberate.	
The error is more than the error correction reporting threshold, but not deliberate.	

A UK registered business sells standard-rated goods to a business customer in France (another EU country).

(c) **Which ONE of the following statements is correct?**

TICK ONE BOX

	✓
As long as the UK business supplies its VAT number to the EU customer the goods will be zero-rated and VAT doesn't need to be charged.	
As long as the EU customer supplies its VAT number to the UK business the goods will be zero-rated and VAT doesn't need to be charged.	
The UK business will charge the French standard VAT rate to the buyer.	
The UK business will charge UK VAT to the customer.	

Task 5

(a) **Identify whether the following statement is true or false.**

TICK ONE BOX

	True	False
When a trader receives a credit note from a supplier VAT payable by the trader will increase.		

The VAT account at the end of a period shows the correct VAT liability of £3,000.00. The VAT return shows a liability of £3,600.00.

(b) Which of the following could explain the difference?

TICK ONE BOX

	✓
Bad debt relief (VAT of £300.00) has been included as output tax rather than input tax on the return.	
A VAT refund from the previous period of £600.00 has been included as input tax on the VAT return.	

Task 6

This task is about preparing figures for a VAT Return for the business of Guy LeBlond.

The business's EU acquisitions are goods that would normally be standard-rated.

The following summaries have been extracted from Guy's accounts over a three month period.

Sales day book summary

	Zero-rated sales £	Standard-rated sales £	VAT £	Total £
UK sales	42,500.00	567,000.00	113,400.00	722,900.00

Purchases day book summary

	Zero-rated purchases £	Standard-rated purchases £	VAT – on UK purchases £	EU acquisitions £	Total £
UK purchases/expenses	4,250.00	150,600.00	30,120.00	25,678.00	210,648.00

(a) Calculate the figure for Box 1 of the VAT Return.

£ [ ]

(b) Calculate the figure for Box 2 of the VAT Return.

£ [ ]

(c) Calculate the figure for Box 4 of the VAT Return.

£ [ ]

Task 7

This task is about completing a VAT return.

The following accounts have been extracted from Bradley Ltd's ledgers for quarter ended 30 June 20X1.

Sales day book summary

	Zero-rated sales £	Standard-rated sales £	VAT £	Total £
UK sales	22,500.00	67,000.00	13,400.00	102,900.00

Purchases day book summary

	Zero-rated purchases £	Standard-rated purchases £	VAT £	Total £
UK purchases/expenses	4,250.00	15,600.00	3,120.00	22,970.00

Sales returns day book summary

	Standard-rated sales £	VAT £	Total £
UK Sales	3,700.00	740.00	4,440.00

Cash payments book summary

	Net £	VAT £	Total £
Cash purchases/expenses	8,550.00	1,710.00	10,260.00

Journal (extract)

	Debit £	Credit £
Irrecoverable (bad) debts expense	5,200.00	
VAT account	1,040.00	
Receivables (debtors) (VAT inclusive at 20%)		6,240.00

Complete Boxes 1 to 9 of the VAT return below for quarter ended 30 June 20X1

VAT return for quarter ended 30 June 20X1		£
VAT due in this period on **sales** and other outputs	**Box 1**	
VAT due in this period on **acquisitions** from other **EC Member States**	**Box 2**	
Total VAT due **(the sum of Boxes 1 and 2)**	**Box 3**	
VAT reclaimed in the period on **purchases** and other inputs, including acquisitions from the EC	**Box 4**	
Net VAT to be paid to HM Revenue & Customs or reclaimed by you **(difference between Boxes 3 and 4)**	**Box 5**	
Total value of **sales** and all other outputs excluding any VAT. **Include your Box 8 figure**	**Box 6**	
Total value of purchases and all other inputs excluding any VAT. **Include your Box 9 figure**	**Box 7**	
Total value of all **supplies** of goods and related costs, excluding any VAT, to other **EC Member States**	**Box 8**	
Total value of all **acquisitions** of goods and related costs, excluding any VAT, from other **EC Member States**	**Box 9**	

Task 8

Reply to Holly Field's email giving her the information she has requested

To: Accounts assistant
From: Holly Field
Subject: Impact of a rise in the VAT rate
Date: 17 July 20X1

I have been listening to the news recently and have heard there may be a rise in the standard rate of VAT from 20% to 25%.

I am extremely concerned as to how this will affect my business. Most of my sales are direct to the general public, so I am unsure whether to increase my prices to take account of the proposed new rate, or to try and keep them the same.

Would you mind explaining the consequences of these two options for me?

Your speedy response would be much appreciated,

Holly

You are required to reply to Holly, filling in the missing details of the email below.

EMAIL

To:	Holly Field
From:	Accounts assistant
Subject:	Impact of a rise in the VAT rate
Date:	20 July 20X1

Dear Holly,

Thank you for your email requesting details of how the proposed rise in the standard rate of VAT might affect your business.

As you quite rightly say, you could [▼] (1) , which means effectively, you as a business will suffer the impact of the increased rate. Alternatively you could [▼] (1) resulting in your customers having to pay extra, which in itself, may lead to the loss of revenue.

For example with the present rate of VAT at 20% if you want to make income of £100 on a sale you will charge your customers £[▼] (2).

With a proposed rise to 25% you can either:

- [▼] (3) to your customer, which will still leave you £100; or

- [▼] (3) for your customers, leaving you only £96 after output VAT is charged (£120 × 100/125).

This is a decision that you will need to give careful thought to, but I hope this clarifies the situation for you.

Kind regards

Accounts Assistant

Picklist:

(1)
could keep your prices the same
increase your prices

(2)
100
120

(3)
charge £125 (£100 plus 25% VAT)
keep your price at £120

BPP PRACTICE ASSESSMENT 3
INDIRECT TAX FA 2018

ANSWERS

Indirect Tax (IDRX)
BPP practice assessment 3

Task 1

(a)

	✓
Register immediately	
Monitor turnover and register later	✓

Taxable supplies to date are £75,000, which is under the compulsory registration threshold

(b)

	✓
Register immediately	✓
Monitor turnover and register later	

As taxable supplies will be approximately £86,500 in the next 30 days, Julian is required to register under the future test

....

Task 2

(a)

	True	False
A business makes supplies that are both standard-rated and zero-rated.		✓
All of the input VAT can be reclaimed providing certain (de minimis) conditions are met.		

The *de minimis* test is applied when a trader makes taxable and **exempt** supplies.

(b)

	✓
15 June 20X1	
20 June 20X1	
23 June 20X1	✓
2 July 20X1	

The basic tax point (delivery date) of 20 June is replaced by the actual tax point (invoice date) of 23 June as the invoice is issued within 14 days of the basic tax point.

(c)

	✓
VAT number of supplier	
Invoice date	
VAT number of customer	✓
Rate of VAT	
Total price excluding VAT for each type of item	
Total amount of VAT for each type of item	
Total price including VAT for each type of item	✓
Name and address of customer	
Name and address of supplier	

Task 3

(a) A business operating the cash accounting scheme will benefit from:

	✓
Only having to submit one VAT return a year	
Automatic bad debt relief	✓
Paying a percentage of turnover over to HMRC	

(b) When a business operates the annual accounting scheme:

	✓
Each year, the business submits one annual return and makes one payment.	
Each year, the business submits one annual return and makes ten payments.	✓
Each year, the business submits one annual return and makes four payments.	

(c) When a business operating the flat rate scheme:

	✓
The business pays a percentage of tax-inclusive turnover to HMRC and reclaims input VAT.	
The business pays a percentage of tax-exclusive turnover to HMRC and reclaims input VAT.	
The business pays a percentage of tax-inclusive turnover to HMRC and cannot reclaim input VAT.	✓
The business pays a percentage of tax-exclusive turnover to HMRC and cannot reclaim input VAT.	

Task 4

(a)

	✓
Brown Ltd must charge an amount of output tax (the fuel scale charge) to reflect the private use.	✓
Brown Ltd must charge an amount of input tax (the fuel scale charge) to reflect the private use.	

(b)

	✓
The error is less than the error correction reporting threshold, but deliberate.	✓
The error is less than the error correction reporting threshold, but not deliberate.	
The error is more than the error correction reporting threshold, and deliberate.	✓
The error is more than the error correction reporting threshold, but not deliberate.	✓

(c)

As long as the UK business supplies its VAT number to the EU customer the goods will be zero-rated and VAT doesn't need to be charged.	
As long as the EU customer supplies its VAT number to the UK business the goods will be zero-rated and VAT doesn't need to be charged.	✓
The UK business will charge the French standard VAT rate to the buyer.	
The UK business will charge UK VAT to the customer.	

Task 5

(a)

	True	False
When a trader receives a credit note from a supplier VAT payable by the trader will increase.	✓	

(b)

Bad debt relief (VAT of £300.00) has been included as output tax rather than input tax on the return.	✓
A VAT refund from the previous period of £600.00 has been included as input tax on the VAT return.	

Task 6

(a) **Box 1 of the VAT Return.**

£	113,400.00

(b) **Box 2 of the VAT Return.**

£	5,135.60

£25,678.00 × 20%

(c) **Box 4 of the VAT Return.**

£	35,255.60

£30,120.00 + £5,135.60

Task 7

VAT return for quarter ended 30 June 20X1		£
VAT due in this period on **sales** and other outputs	**Box 1**	12,660.00
VAT due in this period on **acquisitions** from other **EC Member States**	**Box 2**	0
Total VAT due **(the sum of Boxes 1 and 2)**	**Box 3**	12,660.00
VAT reclaimed in the period on **purchases** and other inputs, including acquisitions from the EC	**Box 4**	5,870.00
Net VAT to be paid to HM Revenue & Customs or reclaimed by you **(difference between Boxes 3 and 4)**	**Box 5**	6,790.00
Total value of **sales** and all other outputs excluding any VAT. **Include your Box 8 figure**	**Box 6**	85,800
Total value of purchases and all other inputs excluding any VAT. **Include your Box 9 figure**	**Box 7**	28,400
Total value of all **supplies** of goods and related costs, excluding any VAT, to other **EC Member States**	**Box 8**	0
Total value of all **acquisitions** of goods and related costs, excluding any VAT, from other **EC Member States**	**Box 9**	0

Workings:

		£
Box 1	Sales day book	13,400.00
	Sales returns day book	(740.00)
		12,660.00
Box 4	Purchases day book	3,120.00
	Cash payments book	1,710.00
	Bad debt relief	1,040.00
		5,870.00
Box 6	Sales day book – standard-rated	67,000.00
	Sales day book – zero-rated	22,500.00
	Sales returns day book	(3,700.00)
		85,800
Box 7	Purchases day book – standard-rated	15,600.00
	Purchases day book – zero-rated	4,250.00
	Cash payments book	8,550.00
		28,400

Task 8

EMAIL

To:	Holly Field
From:	Accounts assistant
Subject:	Impact of a rise in the VAT rate
Date:	20 July 20X1

Dear Holly,

Thank you for your email requesting details of how the proposed rise in the standard rate of VAT might affect your business.

As you quite rightly say, you can keep your prices the same , which means effectively, you as a business will suffer the impact of the increased rate. Alternatively you could increase your prices , resulting in your customers having to pay extra, which in itself, may lead to the loss of revenue.

For example with the present rate of VAT at 20% if you want to make income of £100 on a sale you will charge your customers £ 120 .

With a proposed rise to 25% you can either:

- charge £125 (£100 plus 25% VAT) to your customer, which will still leave you £100; or

- keep your price at £120 for your customers, leaving you only £96 after output VAT is charged (£120 × 100/125).

This is a decision that you will need to give careful thought to, but I hope this clarifies the situation for you.

Kind regards

Accounts Assistant

* *

Tax reference material FA 2018

Introduction

This document comprises data that you may need to consult during your Indirect Tax computer-based assessment.

The material can be consulted during the sample and live assessments through pop-up windows. It is made available here so you can familiarise yourself with the content before the test.

Do not take a print of this document into the exam room with you*.

This document may be changed to reflect periodical updates in the computer-based assessment, so please check you have the most recent version while studying. This version is based on Finance Act 2018 and is for use in AAT assessments 1 January – 31 December 2019.

*Unless you need a printed version as part of reasonable adjustments for particular needs, in which case you must discuss this with your tutor at least six weeks before the assessment date.

Contents

Introduction to VAT

VAT is a tax that's charged on most goods and services that VAT-registered businesses provide in the UK. It's also charged on goods and some services that are imported from countries outside the European Union (EU), and brought into the UK from other EU countries.

VAT is charged when a VAT-registered business sells taxable goods and services to either another business or to a non-business customer. This is called output tax.

When a VAT-registered business buys taxable goods or services for business use it can generally reclaim the VAT it has paid. This is called input tax.

Her Majesty's Revenue and Customs (HMRC) is the government department responsible for operating the VAT system. Payments of VAT collected are made by VAT-registered businesses to HMRC.

Rates of VAT

There are three rates of VAT, depending on the goods or services the business provides. The rates are:

- Standard – 20%. The standard-rate VAT fraction for calculating the VAT Element of a gross supply is 20/120 or 1/6

- Reduced – 5%.

- Zero – 0%.

There are also some goods and services that are:

- Exempt from VAT
- Outside the scope of VAT (outside the UK VAT system altogether)

Taxable supplies

Zero-rated goods and services count as taxable supplies and are part of taxable turnover, but no VAT is added to the selling price because the VAT rate is 0%.

If the business sells goods and services that are exempt, no VAT is added as they're not taxable supplies and they're also not taxable turnover.

Generally, a business can't register for VAT or reclaim the VAT on purchases if it only sells exempt goods and services. Where some of its supplies are of exempt goods and services, the business is referred to as partially exempt. It may not be able to reclaim the VAT on all of its purchases.

A business which buys and sells only - or mainly - zero-rated goods or services can apply to HMRC to be exempt from registering for VAT. This could make sense if the business pays little or no VAT on purchases.

Taxable turnover

Taxable turnover consists of standard-rated sales plus all reduced-rated and zero-rated sales but excludes the VAT on those sales, exempt sales and out-of-scope sales. If one VAT-registered business acquires another business it immediately absorbs the turnover of that business, whether the acquired business is registered for VAT or not. All VAT decisions must thereafter be made based on the combined turnover.

Change in VAT rate

Generally a business must use the VAT rate applicable from the time of the legislative change, unless payment has already been received or the goods have already been delivered. In these cases a tax point has already been created and the rate applicable will have been set by the tax point.

An exception arises where the goods have been delivered, or otherwise removed by the customer, the supplier has elected to follow the 14-day rule for issuing VAT

invoices and the VAT rate increases between the date of delivery of the goods and the issuing of the invoice. In this case it is the new VAT rate which applies.

Immediately after the rate change a business may opt to honour supplies of goods and services at the rate which applied when the contract to supply was agreed, however output tax is still accountable at the new rate.

If the business offers a prompt payment discount and opts to issue a credit note to cover the reduction in payment made by the customer then a change in VAT rate which occurs between the issue of the original invoice and final payment will not be affected by the change in VAT rate. The rate due on the credit note, issued to account for the reduced payment made, will be fixed by the tax point of the original invoice.

Registration and deregistration

Registration threshold

If, as at the end of any month, taxable turnover for the previous 12 months is more than the current registration threshold of £85,000, the business must register for VAT within 30 days. Registration without delay is required if, at any time, the value of taxable turnover in the next 30 day period alone is expected to be more than the registration threshold.

A business which has trading that temporarily takes it above the VAT threshold of £85,000 but which expects turnover to drop back below the threshold almost immediately can apply to stay unregistered, but the business must be able to prove to HMRC that the momentary increase is a true one-off occurrence.

If trading is below the registration threshold

If taxable turnover hasn't crossed the registration threshold, the business can still apply to register for VAT voluntarily.

Deregistration threshold

The deregistration threshold is £83,000. If taxable turnover for the previous 12 months is less than or equal to £83,000, or if it is expected to fall to £83,000 or less in the next 12 months, the business can either:

- Voluntarily remain registered for VAT, or
- Ask HMRC for its VAT registration to be cancelled

Failure to register

A business which fails to register when it is required to do so may face a civil penalty. More importantly HMRC will treat the business as though it had registered on time and will expect VAT to be accounted for as if it had been charged. The business has two choices in respect of this VAT, which it has not included in its invoices.

It may either:

- Allow HMRC to treat the invoices as VAT inclusive and absorb the VAT which should have been charged, OR

- Account for VAT as an addition to the charges already invoiced and attempt to recover this VAT from its customers.

Cancellation of VAT registration

A registration must be cancelled if the business is closed down or ceases to make taxable supplies.

If a business is being taken over by a business with a completely different structure, for example an unincorporated business being taken over by an incorporated business or vice versa, the original registration must be cancelled. It will either be

replaced by a new registration for the new business, or be subsumed into the registration of the expanded business. In some circumstances the new business may apply for the registration of the business being taken over to be re-allocated to the new business. This may happen because two businesses merge and only one is currently registered. Re-allocation of the existing registration may be the most appropriate method of dealing with VAT registration.

Changes to the VAT registration

Some business changes will necessitate a change in details of the VAT registration, such as a change in the trading name or the address of the business. Other reasons for changes to the registration are a change in main business activities, particularly if this means a significant change to the types of supply, and changes to the business bank account details.

Failure to notify HMRC of changes which either cancel or change registration within 30 days of the relevant change may render the business and its owners liable to a civil penalty.

Keeping business records and VAT records

All VAT-registered businesses must keep certain business and VAT records.

These records are not required to be kept in a set way, provided they:

- Are complete and up to date

- Allow the correct amount of VAT owed to HMRC or by HMRC to be worked out

- Are easily accessible when an HMRC visit takes place, eg the figures used to fill in the VAT Return must be easy to find

Business records

Business records which must be kept include the following:

- Annual accounts, including statements of profit or loss
- Bank statements and paying-in slips
- Cash books and other account books
- Orders and delivery notes
- Purchases and sales day books
- Records of daily takings such as till rolls
- Relevant business correspondence

VAT records

In addition to these business records, VAT records must be kept.

In general, the business must keep the following VAT records:

- Records of all the standard-rated, reduced-rated, zero-rated and exempt goods and services that are bought and sold.

- Copies of all sales invoices issued. However, businesses do not have to keep copies of any less detailed (simplified) VAT invoices for items under £250 including VAT

- All purchase invoices for items purchased for business purposes unless the gross value of the supply is £25 or less and the purchase was from a coin-operated telephone or vending machine, or for car parking charges or tolls.

- All credit notes and debit notes received.

- Copies of all credit notes and debit notes issued.

- Records of any goods or services bought for which there is no VAT reclaim, such as business entertainment.

- Records of any goods exported.

- Any adjustments, such as corrections to the accounts or amended VAT invoices.

Generally all business records that are relevant for VAT must be kept for at least six years. If this causes serious problems in terms of storage or costs, then HMRC may allow some records to be kept for a shorter period. Records may be stored digitally especially if that is needed to overcome storage and access difficulties.

Keeping a VAT account

A VAT account is the separate record that must be kept of the VAT charged on taxable sales (referred to as output tax or VAT payable) and the VAT paid on purchases (called input tax or VAT reclaimable). It provides the link between the business records and the VAT Return. A VAT-registered business needs to add up the VAT in the sales and purchases records and then transfer these totals to the VAT account, using separate headings for VAT payable and VAT reclaimable.

The VAT account can be kept in whatever way suits the business best, as long as it includes information about the VAT that it:

- Owes on sales, including when fuel scale charges are used
- Owes on acquisitions from other European Union (EU) countries
- Owes following a correction or error adjustment
- Can reclaim on business purchases
- Can reclaim on acquisitions from other EU countries
- Can reclaim following a correction or error adjustment
- Is reclaiming via VAT bad debt relief

The business must also keep records of any adjustments that have been made, such as balancing payments for the annual accounting scheme for VAT.

Information from the VAT account can be used to complete the VAT Return at the end of each accounting period. VAT reclaimable is subtracted from the VAT payable, to give the net amount of VAT to pay to or reclaim from HMRC.

Unless it is using the cash accounting scheme, a business:

- Must pay the VAT charged on invoices to customers during the accounting period that relates to the return, even if those customers have not paid the invoices

- May reclaim the VAT charged on invoices from suppliers during the accounting period that relates to the return, even if it has not paid the invoices.

Exempt and partly-exempt businesses

Exempt goods and services

There are some goods and services on which VAT is not charged.

Exempt supplies are not taxable for VAT, so sales of exempt goods and services are not included in taxable turnover for VAT purposes. If a registered business buys exempt items, there is no VAT to reclaim.

(This is different to zero-rated supplies. In both cases VAT is not added to the selling price, but zero-rated goods or services are taxable for VAT at 0%, and are included in taxable turnover.)

Businesses which only sell or supply exempt goods or services

A business which only supplies goods or services that are exempt from VAT is called an exempt business. It cannot register for VAT, so it won't be able to reclaim any input tax on business purchases.

(Again this is different to zero-rated supplies, as a business can reclaim the input tax on any purchases that relate to zero-rated sales. In addition, a business which sells mainly or only zero-rated items may apply for an exemption from VAT registration, but then it can't claim back any input tax.)

Reclaiming VAT in a partly-exempt business

A business that is registered for VAT but that makes some exempt supplies is referred to as partly, or partially, exempt.

Generally, such businesses won't be able to reclaim the input tax paid on purchases that relate to exempt supplies.

However if the amount of input tax incurred relating to exempt supplies is below a minimum *de minimus* amount, input tax can be reclaimed in full.

If the amount of input tax incurred relating to exempt supplies is above the *de minimus* amount, only the part of the input tax that related to non-exempt supplies can be reclaimed.

Place of supply

Businesses which make supplies of goods and services to other member states of the EU or to countries outside the EU, or which receive goods and services from other member states of the EU or from countries outside the EU, must apply the 'place of supply' rules for both goods and services. Place of supply is important because it drives the amount of VAT, if any, which is to be added to the cost of the services, and the manner in which any VAT is accounted for.

The place of supply is the place, or country, where the supply is made.

The following rules apply to a supplier based in the UK, with no alternative location elsewhere in the EU or outside the EU.

Supplies and receipts of goods

The place of supply for goods is always the country where the goods originate. This applies whether the goods are for the enjoyment of a business customer or a domestic customer.

Supplies and receipts of services

Supplies of services are covered by the 'Place of supply of services order' or POSSO. Here the place of supply can be different depending on who the customer is, and whether the supply of services is within, or outside, the EU.

When the customer is a business customer the place of supply is where the customer is.

Should the customer be either:

• A non-business,
• An unregistered business, or
• A registered business, but the supply is of a non-business nature

then the place of supply is the country where the supplier is, irrespective of where the customer is.

Tax points

The time of supply, known as the 'tax point', is the date when a transaction takes place for VAT purposes. This date is not necessarily the date the supply physically takes place.

Generally, a registered business must pay or reclaim VAT in the (usually quarterly) VAT period, or tax period, in which the time of supply occurs, and it must use the correct rate of VAT in force on that date. This means knowing the time of supply/tax point for every transaction is important, as it must be put on the right VAT Return.

Time of supply (tax point) for goods and services

The time of supply for VAT purposes is defined as follows:

- For transactions where no VAT invoice is issued, the time of supply is normally the date the supply takes place (as defined below).

- For transactions where there is a VAT invoice, the time of supply is normally the date the invoice is issued, even if this is after the date the supply took place (as defined below).

To issue a VAT invoice, it must be sent (by post, email etc) or given to the customer for them to keep. A tax point cannot be created simply by preparing an invoice.

However there are exceptions to these rules on time of supply, detailed below.

Date the supply takes place

For goods, the time when the goods are considered to be supplied for VAT purposes is the date when one of the following happens:

- The supplier sends the goods to the customer.

- The customer collects the goods from the supplier.

- The goods (which are not either sent or collected) are made available for the customer to use, for example if the supplier is assembling something on the customer's premises.

For services, the date when the services are supplied for VAT purposes is the date when the service is carried out and all the work – except invoicing – is finished.

Exceptions regarding time of supply (tax point)

The above general principles for working out the time of supply do not apply in the following situations:

- For transactions where a VAT invoice is issued, or payment is received, in advance of the date of supply, the time of supply is the date the invoice is issued or the payment is received, whichever is the earlier.

- If the supplier receives full payment before the date when the supply takes place and no VAT invoice has yet been issued, the time of supply is the date the payment is received.

- If the supplier receives part-payment before the date when the supply takes place, the time of supply becomes the date the part-payment is received but only for the amount of the part-payment (assuming no VAT invoice has been issued before this date – in which case the time of supply is the date the invoice is issued). The time of supply for the remainder will follow the normal rules – and might fall in a different VAT period, and so have to go onto a different VAT Return.

- If the supplier issues a VAT invoice more than 14 days after the date when the supply took place, the time of supply will be the date the supply took place, and not the date the invoice is issued. However, if a supplier has genuine commercial difficulties in invoicing within 14 days of the supply taking place, they can contact HMRC to ask for permission to issue invoices later than 14 days and move the time of supply to this later date.

- Where services are being supplied on a continuous basis over a period in excess of a month but invoices are being issued regularly throughout the period. A tax point is created every time an invoice is issued or a payment is made, whichever happens first. A business may issue invoices for a whole 12 month period but only if it is known that payments will be made regularly.

- Goods supplied to a customer on a sale or return basis remain the property of the supplier until the customer indicates they are intending to keep them. If a time limit has been fixed for the sale or return the tax point is:

    - Where the fixed period is 12 months or less – the date the time limit expires

    - Where the fixed period is more than 12 months, or there is no fixed period – 12 months from the date the goods were sent

    - Where the customer adopts the goods before the fixed period has expired – the date the goods are adopted.

A payment made, which is not returnable, normally indicates that the goods have been adopted, however the receipt of a deposit which is repayable if the goods are returned is not an indication of adoption.

VAT invoices

To whom is a VAT invoice issued?

Whenever a VAT-registered business supplies taxable goods or services to another VAT-registered business, it must give the customer a VAT invoice.

A VAT-registered business is not required to issue a VAT invoice to a non-registered business or to a member of the public, but it must do so if requested.

What is a VAT invoice?

A VAT invoice shows certain VAT details of a supply of goods or services. It can be either in paper or electronic form. An electronic invoice (e-invoice) is only valid if it is in a secure format, for example a 'pdf'.

A VAT-registered customer must have a valid VAT invoice from the supplier in order to claim back the VAT they have paid on the purchase for their business.

What is NOT a VAT invoice?

The following are NOT VAT invoices:

- Proforma invoices
- Invoices for only zero-rated or exempt supplies
- Invoices that state 'this is not a VAT invoice'
- Statements of account
- Delivery notes
- Orders
- Letters, emails or other correspondence

A registered business cannot reclaim the VAT it has paid on a purchase by using these documents as proof of payment.

What a VAT invoice must show

A VAT invoice must show:

- An invoice number which is unique and follows on from the number of the previous invoice – any spoiled or cancelled serially numbered invoice must be kept to show to a VAT officer at the next VAT inspection

- The seller's name or trading name, and address

- The seller's VAT registration number

- The invoice date

- The time of supply or tax point if this is different from the invoice date

- The customer's name or trading name, and address

- A description sufficient to identify the goods or services supplied to the customer

For each different type of item listed on the invoice, the business must show:

- The unit price or rate, excluding VAT
- The quantity of goods or the extent of the services
- The rate of VAT that applies to what is being sold
- The total amount payable, excluding VAT
- The rate of any cash or settlement discount
- The total amount of VAT charged

If the business issues a VAT invoice that includes zero-rated or exempt goods or services, it must:

- Show clearly that there is no VAT payable on those goods or services
- Show the total of those values separately

Where a prompt payment discount (PPD) is offered VAT must be accounted for to HMRC on the actual consideration received. The business must decide how to express this on the invoice. It may:

- Invoice at the discounted value with VAT on that amount and then issue an additional invoice for the discount plus VAT at the point it becomes clear the customer will not take the discount by paying within the prompt payment period, OR

- Invoice for the full value with VAT on that amount and then issue a credit note for the discount plus VAT should the customer pay the discounted value within the prompt payment period, OR

- Invoice for the full value of the supply and associated VAT but provide information to the customer which allows it to determine how much to pay if they make payment within the prompt payment discount period. This information must include details of the input tax which they are permitted to recover depending on when they make payment. A warning should be included to the customer that failure to account for the correct amount of VAT is an offence.

Rounding on VAT invoices

The total VAT payable on all goods and services shown on a VAT invoice may be rounded down to a whole penny. Any fraction of a penny can be ignored. (This concession is not available to retailers.)

Time limits for issuing VAT invoices

There is a strict time limit on issuing VAT invoices. Normally a VAT invoice to a VAT-registered customer must be issued within 30 days of the basic tax point, which is either the date of supply of the goods or services, subject to the 14 day rule or, if the business was paid in advance, the date payment was received. This is so the customer can claim back the VAT on the supply, if they are entitled to do so.

The 30 day limit for goods starts with the day the goods are sent to the customer or taken by the customer or made available to the customer.

Invoices cannot be issued any later without permission from HMRC, except in a few limited circumstances.

A valid VAT invoice is needed to reclaim VAT

Even if a business is registered for VAT, it can normally only reclaim VAT on purchases if:

- They are for use in the business or for business purposes and
- A valid VAT invoice for the purchase is received and retained*.

*Subject to the rules for VAT invoices for supplies of £250 or less including VAT and for supplies of £25 including VAT or less:

- A simplified invoice for supplies of £250 or less is acceptable as a 'valid VAT invoice' for input tax reclaim.

- Supplies of £25 or less including VAT, supported by a simple till receipt, can be assumed to be acceptable as a 'valid VAT invoice' for input tax reclaim as long as the business has a reasonable understanding that the supplier is VAT registered.

Only VAT-registered businesses can issue valid VAT invoices. A business cannot reclaim VAT on any goods or services that are purchased from a business that is not VAT-registered.

Where simplified (less detailed) VAT invoices can be issued

Simplified VAT invoices

If a VAT-registered business makes taxable supplies of goods or services for £250 or less including VAT, then it can issue a simplified (less detailed) VAT invoice that only needs to show:

- The seller's name and address
- The seller's VAT registration number
- The time of supply (tax point)
- A description of the goods or services
- The total payable including VAT

If the supply includes items at different VAT rates then, for each different VAT rate, the simplified VAT invoice must also show the VAT rate applicable to the item(s).

Exempt supplies must not be included on a simplified VAT invoice.

There is no requirement for the business making the supply to keep copies of any less detailed invoices it has issued.

Proforma invoices

If there is a need to issue a sales document for goods or services not supplied yet, the business can issue a 'proforma' invoice or a similar document as part of the offer to supply goods or services to customers.

A proforma invoice is not a VAT invoice, and it should be clearly marked with the words 'This is not a VAT invoice'.

If a potential customer accepts the goods or services offered to them and these are actually supplied, then a VAT invoice must be issued within the appropriate time limit if appropriate.

If the business has been issued with a proforma invoice by a supplier it cannot be used to claim back VAT on the purchase. A VAT invoice must be obtained from the supplier.

Advance payments or deposits

An advance payment, or deposit, is a proportion of the total selling price that a customer pays before they are supplied with goods or services. When a business asks for an advance payment or deposit, the tax point is whichever of the following happens first:

- The date a VAT invoice is issued for the advance payment
- The date the advance payment is received

The business must include the VAT on the advance payment or deposit on the VAT Return for the period when the tax point occurs.

If the customer pays any remaining balance before the goods are delivered or the services are performed, another tax point is created when whichever of the following happens first:

- A VAT invoice is issued for the balance
- Payment of the balance is received

The VAT on the balance must be included on the VAT Return for the period when the tax point occurs.

VAT does not have to be accounted for if a deposit is either:

- Refunded to the customer in full when they return goods safely, or
- Kept as compensation for loss of or damage to the goods.

Discounts on goods and services

If any goods or services supplied by a VAT-registered business are subject to a trade, bulk or other form of discount, VAT is charged on the VAT invoice on the discounted price rather than the full price.

Returned goods, credit notes, debit notes and VAT

For a buyer who has received a VAT invoice

If goods are returned to the seller for full or partial credit there are three options:

- Return the invoice to the supplier and obtain a replacement invoice showing the proper amount of VAT due, if any

- Obtain a credit note from the supplier

- Issue a debit note to the supplier

If the buyer issues a debit note or receives a credit note, it must:

- Record this in the accounting records

- Enter it on the next VAT Return, deducting the VAT on the credit or debit note from the amount of VAT which can be reclaimed

For a seller who has issued a VAT invoice

If goods are returned by a customer, there are again three options:

- Cancel and recover the original invoice, and issue a replacement showing the correct amount of any VAT due, if any

- Issue a credit note to the customer

- Obtain a debit note from the customer

If the seller issues a credit note or receives a debit note, it must:

- Record this in the accounting records

- Enter it on the next VAT Return, deducting the VAT on the credit or debit note from the amount of VAT payable

Entertainment expenses

Business entertainment

Business entertainment is any form of free or subsidised entertainment or hospitality to non-employees, for example suppliers and customers. Generally a business cannot reclaim input tax on business entertainment expenses. The exception is that input tax can be reclaimed in respect of entertaining overseas customers, but not UK or Isle of Man customers.

Employee expenses and entertainment

The business can, however, reclaim VAT on employee expenses and employee entertainment expenses if those expenses relate to travel and subsistence or where the entertainment applies only to employees.

When the entertainment is in respect of a mixed group of both employees and non-employees (eg customers and/or suppliers), the business can only reclaim VAT on the proportion of the expenses that is for employees and on the proportion for overseas customers.

Vehicles and motoring expenses

VAT and vehicles

When it buys a car a registered business generally cannot reclaim the VAT. There are some exceptions – for example, when the car is used mainly as one of the following:

- A taxi
- For driving instruction
- For self-drive hire

If the VAT on the original purchase price of a car bought new is not reclaimed, the business does not have to charge any VAT when it is sold. This is because the sale of the car is exempt for VAT purposes. If the business did reclaim the VAT when it bought the car new, VAT is chargeable when it comes to sell it.

VAT-registered businesses can generally reclaim the VAT when they buy a commercial vehicle such as a van, lorry or tractor.

Reclaiming VAT on road fuel

If the business pays for road fuel, it can deal with the VAT charged on the fuel in one of four ways:

- Reclaim all of the VAT. All of the fuel must be used only for business purposes.

- Reclaim all of the VAT and pay the appropriate fuel scale charge - this is a way of accounting for output tax on fuel that the business buys but that is then used for private motoring.

- Reclaim only the VAT that relates to fuel used for business mileage. Detailed records of business and private mileage must be kept.

- Do not reclaim any VAT. This can be a useful option if mileage is low and also if fuel is used for both business and private motoring. If the business chooses this option it must apply it to all vehicles, including commercial vehicles.

Transactions outside the UK

Exports, despatches and supplying goods abroad: charging VAT

If a business sells, supplies or transfers goods out of the UK to someone in another country it may need to charge VAT on them.

VAT on exports of goods to non-EU countries

Generally speaking, the business can zero-rate supplies exported outside the EU, provided it follows strict rules, obtains and keeps the necessary evidence, and obeys all laws.

The term 'exports' is reserved to describe sales to a country outside the EU. Goods supplied to another EU member state are technically known as despatches rather than exports.

VAT on despatches of goods to someone who is not VAT registered in another EU member state

When a business supplies goods to someone in another EU member state, and they are not registered for VAT in that country, it should normally charge VAT.

VAT on despatches of goods to someone who is VAT registered in another EU member state

If, however, goods are supplied to someone who is registered for VAT in the destination EU member state, the business can zero-rate the supply for VAT purposes, provided it meets certain conditions.

Imports, acquisitions and purchasing goods from abroad: paying and reclaiming VAT

Generally speaking, VAT is payable on all purchases of goods that are bought from abroad at the same rate that would apply to the goods if bought in the UK. The business must tell HMRC about goods that it imports, and pay any VAT and duty that is due.

VAT on imports of goods from non-EU countries

VAT may be charged on imports of goods bought from non-EU countries. The business can reclaim any VAT paid on the goods imported as input tax.

VAT on goods acquired from EU member states

If a business is registered for VAT in the UK and buys goods from inside the EU, these are known as acquisitions rather than imports. Usually no VAT is charged by the supplier but acquisition tax, at the same rate of VAT that would apply if the goods were supplied in the UK, is due on the acquisition. This is included in Box 2 of the VAT return. It can be reclaimed as input tax in Box 4 of the VAT return as if the goods were bought in the UK.

Bad debts

When a business can reclaim VAT on bad debts

VAT that has been paid to HMRC and which has not been received from the customer can be reclaimed as bad debt relief. The conditions are that:

- The debt is more than six months and less than four years and six months old

- The debt has been written off in the VAT account and transferred to a separate bad debt account

- The debt has not been sold or handed to a factoring company

- The business did not charge more than the normal selling price for the items

Bad debt relief does not apply when the cash accounting scheme is used because the VAT is not paid to HMRC until after the customer has paid it to the supplier.

How to claim bad debt relief

If the business is entitled to claim bad debt relief, add the amount of VAT to be reclaimed to the amount of VAT being reclaimed on purchases (input tax) and put the total figure in Box 4 of the VAT Return.

Effect of a change in the business

If a business closes down, relief for all outstanding bad debts up to and including the date of closure will need to be claimed, if eligible.

Where a business is acquired as a going concern and the acquiring business takes on the VAT registration of the closing business, it may be possible to transfer the outstanding bad debts from the old to the new business.

Completing the online VAT Return, box by box

The online VAT Return is completed as follows:

Box 1 – VAT due in this period on sales and other outputs

- This is the total amount of VAT charged on sales to customers. It also has to include VAT due to HMRC for other reasons, for example fuel scale charges.

- Include VAT due on a supply of services from another member state of the EC, where the supplier has 'zero-rated' the supply.

Box 2 – VAT due in this period on acquisitions from other EC Member States

- VAT due, but not yet paid, on goods bought from other EU member states, and any services directly related to those goods (such as delivery charges). The business may be able to reclaim this amount, and if so it must be included in the total in Box 4.

Box 3 – Total VAT due (the sum of boxes 1 and 2). This is calculated automatically by the online return

Box 4 – VAT reclaimed in this period on purchases and other inputs (including acquisitions from the EC)

- This is the VAT charged on purchases for use in the business. It should also include:

  - VAT paid on imports from countries outside the EC

  - VAT due (but not yet paid) on goods from other EC member states, and any services directly related to those goods (such as delivery charges) - this is the figure in Box 2.

  - VAT due on a supply of services from a supplier in another member state of the EC where that supply has been 'zero-rated' by the supplier. This will be the same amount as entered in Box 1 in respect of the same transaction.

Box 5 – Net VAT to be paid to HM Revenue & Customs or reclaimed by you (difference between boxes 3 and 4). This is calculated automatically by the online return

Box 6 – Total value of sales and all other outputs excluding any VAT. Include your box 8 figure.

- Enter the total figure for sales (excluding VAT) for the period, that is the sales on which the VAT entered in Box 1 was based. Additionally, also include:

  - any zero-rated and exempt sales or other supplies made
  - any amount entered in Box 8
  - exports to outside the EC.

The net amount of any credit notes issued, or debit notes received, is deducted.

Box 7 – Total value of purchases and all other inputs excluding any VAT. Include your box 9 figure.

- Enter the total figure for purchases (excluding VAT) for the period, that is the purchases on which the VAT entered in Box 4 was based. Additionally, also include:
  - any zero-rated and exempt purchases
  - any amount entered in Box 9
  - imports from outside the EU.

Box 8 – Total value of all supplies of goods and related costs, excluding any VAT, to other EC Member States.

- Enter the total value of goods supplied to another EC member state and services related to those goods (such as delivery charges).

Box 9 – Total value of all acquisitions of goods and related costs, excluding any VAT, from other EC Member States.

- Enter the total value of goods received from VAT registered suppliers in another EC member state and services related to those goods (such as delivery charges).

VAT periods, submitting returns and paying VAT

VAT Returns for transactions to the end of the relevant VAT period must be submitted by the due date shown on the VAT Return. VAT due must also be paid by the due date.

What is a VAT period?

A VAT period is the period of time over which the business records VAT transactions in the VAT account for completion of the VAT Return. The VAT period is three months (a quarter) unless the annual accounting scheme is used. The end dates of a business's four VAT periods are determined when it first registers for VAT, but it can choose to amend the dates on which its VAT periods end. This is often done to match VAT periods to accounting period ends.

Submitting VAT Returns online and paying HMRC electronically

It is mandatory for virtually all VAT-registered traders to submit their VAT Returns to HMRC using online filing, and to pay HMRC electronically.

Due dates for submitting the VAT Return and paying electronically

Businesses are responsible for calculating how much VAT they owe and for paying VAT so that the amount clears to HMRC's bank account on or before the due date. Paying on time avoids having to pay a surcharge for late payment.

The normal due date for submitting each VAT Return and electronically paying HMRC any VAT that is owed is one calendar month after the end of the relevant VAT period, unless the annual accounting scheme is operated. The normal due date for the return and payment can be found on the return.

Online filing and electronic payment mean that businesses get an extended due date for filing the return of seven extra calendar days after the normal due date shown on the VAT Return. This extra seven days also applies to paying HMRC so that the amount has cleared into HMRC's bank account. However this does not apply if the business uses the Annual Accounting Scheme for VAT.

If the business pays HMRC by Direct Debit, HMRC automatically collects payment from the business's bank account three bank working days after the extra seven calendar days following the normal due date.

If the business fails to pay cleared funds into HMRC's bank account by the payment deadline, or fails to have sufficient funds in its account to meet the direct debit, it may be liable to a surcharge for late payment.

Repayment of VAT

If the amount of VAT reclaimed (entered in Box 4) is more than the VAT to be paid (entered in Box 3), then the net VAT value in Box 5 is a repayment due to the business from HMRC.

HMRC is obliged to schedule this sum for repayment automatically, provided checks applied to the VAT Return do not indicate that such a repayment might not be due. There may be circumstances when the business does not receive the repayment automatically, for instance if there is an outstanding debt owed to HMRC.

Special accounting schemes

Annual Accounting Scheme for VAT

Using standard VAT accounting, four VAT Returns each year are required. Any VAT due is payable quarterly, and any VAT refunds due are also receivable quarterly.

Using the normal annual accounting scheme, the business makes nine interim payments at monthly intervals. There is only one VAT Return to complete, at the end of the year, when either a balancing payment is payable or a balancing refund is receivable.

Businesses can start on the annual accounting scheme if their estimated taxable turnover during the next tax year is not more than £1.35 million. Businesses already using the annual accounting scheme can continue to do so until the estimated taxable turnover for the next tax year exceeds £1.6 million. If the business is taken over as a going concern the acquiring business must assess the use of the annual accounting scheme in the context of the expected and combined turnover of the new business, and must immediately cease using the scheme if that is expected to exceed £1.6 million.

Whilst using the annual accounting scheme the business may also be able to use either the cash accounting scheme or the flat rate scheme, but not both.

Benefits of annual accounting

- One VAT Return per year, instead of four.

- Two months after the tax period end to complete and send in the annual VAT Return and pay the balance of VAT payable, rather than the usual one month.

- Better management of cash flow by paying a fixed amount in nine instalments.

- Ability to make additional payments as and when required.

- Join from VAT registration day, or at any other time if already registered for VAT.

Disadvantages of annual accounting

- Only one repayment per year, which is not beneficial if the business regularly requires refunds.

- If turnover decreases, interim payments may be higher than the VAT payments would be under standard VAT accounting – again there is a need to wait until the end of the year to receive a refund.

Cash Accounting Scheme for VAT

Using standard VAT accounting, VAT is paid on sales within a VAT period whether or not the customer has paid. VAT is reclaimed on purchases whether or not the business has paid the supplier.

Using cash accounting, VAT is not paid until the customer has paid the invoice. If a customer never pays, the business never has to pay the VAT. VAT is reclaimed on purchases only when the business has paid the invoice.

Cash accounting can be used if the estimated taxable turnover during the next tax year is not more than £1.35 million. A business can continue to use cash accounting until its taxable turnover exceeds £1.6 million.

The cash accounting scheme may be used in conjunction with the annual accounting scheme but not with the flat rate scheme. If the business is taken over as a going concern the acquiring business must assess the use of the cash accounting scheme in the context of the expected and combined turnover of the new business, and must immediately cease using the scheme if that is expected to exceed £1.6 million.

Benefits of cash accounting

Using cash accounting may help cash flow, especially if customers are slow payers. Payment of VAT is not made until the business has received payment from the customer, so if a customer never pays, VAT does not have to be paid on that bad debt as long as the business is using the cash accounting scheme.

Disadvantages of cash accounting

Using cash accounting may adversely affect cash flow:

- The business cannot reclaim VAT on purchases until it has paid for them. This can be a disadvantage if most goods and services are purchased on credit.

- Businesses which regularly reclaim more VAT than they pay will usually receive repayment later under cash accounting than under standard VAT accounting, unless they pay for everything at the time of purchase.

- If a business starts using cash accounting when it starts trading, it will not be able to reclaim VAT on most start-up expenditure, such as initial stock, tools or machinery, until it has actually paid for those items.

- When it leaves the cash accounting scheme the business will have to account for all outstanding VAT due, including on any bad debts.

Flat Rate Scheme for VAT

If its VAT-exclusive taxable turnover is less than £150,000 per year, the business could simplify its VAT accounting by registering on the Flat Rate Scheme and calculating VAT payments as a percentage of its total VAT-inclusive turnover. There

is no reclaim of VAT on purchases - this is taken into account in calculating the flat rate percentage that applies to the business.

The VAT flat rate the business uses usually depends on its business type. It may pay a different rate if it only spends a small amount on goods.

Limited cost business

The business is classed as a 'limited cost business' if its goods cost less than either:

- 2% of its turnover
- £1,000 a year (if its costs are more than 2%)

This means the business pays a flat rate of 16.5%, whatever its business type.

Non-limited cost businesses use their business type to determine the applicable flat rate.

Reclaim of VAT on capital expenditure goods

If the business uses the Flat Rate Scheme, it can reclaim the VAT it has been charged on a single purchase of capital expenditure goods where the amount of the purchase, including VAT, is £2,000 or more.

These capital expenditure goods are dealt with outside the Flat Rate Scheme. This means that the input tax is claimed in box 4 of the VAT return. If the supply is:

- More than one purchase
- Under £2,000 including VAT, or
- Of services

then no VAT is claimable, as this input tax is already taken into account in the calculation of the flat rate percentage.

The flat rate scheme can reduce the time needed in accounting for and working out VAT. Even though the business still needs to show a VAT amount on each VAT invoice issued, it does not need to record how much VAT it charged on every sale in its ledger accounts. Nor does it need to record the VAT paid on every purchase.

Once on the scheme, the business can continue to use it until its total business income exceeds £230,000. If the business is taken over as a going concern the acquiring business must assess the use of the flat rate scheme in the context of the expected and combined turnover of the new business, and must immediately cease using the scheme if that is expected to exceed £230,000. The flat rate scheme may be used in conjunction with the annual accounting scheme but not the cash accounting scheme.

Benefits of using the flat rate scheme

Using the flat rate scheme can save time and smooth cash flow. It offers these benefits:

- No need to record the VAT charged on every sale and purchase, as with standard VAT accounting. This can save time. But although the business only

has to pay HMRC a percentage of its turnover, it must still show VAT at the appropriate normal rate (standard, reduced or zero) on the VAT invoices it issues.

- A first year discount. A business in its first year of VAT registration gets a 1% reduction in the applicable flat rate percentage until the day before the first anniversary of VAT registration.

- Fewer rules to follow, for instance no longer having to work out what VAT on purchases can or cannot be reclaimed.

- Peace of mind, less chance of mistakes and fewer worries about getting the VAT right.

- Certainty. The business always knows what percentage of takings has to be paid to HMRC.

Potential disadvantages of using the flat rate scheme

The flat rate percentages are calculated in a way that takes into account zero-rated and exempt sales. They also contain an allowance for the VAT spent on purchases. So the VAT Flat Rate Scheme might not be right for the business if:

- It buys mostly standard-rated items, as there is no reclaim of any VAT on purchases;

- It regularly receives a VAT repayment under standard VAT accounting;

- It makes a lot of zero-rated or exempt sales; or

- It is a 'limited cost business'.

Errors in previous VAT Returns

Action to be taken at the end of the VAT period

At the end of the VAT period, the business should calculate the net value of all the errors and omissions found during the period that relate to VAT Returns already submitted – that is, any tax which should have been claimed back is subtracted from any additional tax due to HMRC, and any tax that should have been paid is added. Any deliberate errors must not be included – these must be separately declared to HMRC.

What the business should do next depends on whether the net value of all the errors is less than or greater than the 'error correction reporting threshold', which is the greater of:

- £10,000

- 1% of the box 6 figure on the VAT Return for the period when the error was discovered – subject to an upper limit of £50,000

If the net value of all the errors is less than the error reporting threshold then, if preferred, the errors may be corrected by making an adjustment on the current VAT Return (Method 1).

However, if the value of the net VAT error discovered is above this threshold, it must be declared to HMRC separately, in writing (Method 2).

How to adjust the VAT Return: Method 1

Errors from previous VAT Returns can be corrected by adjusting the VAT amounts on the current VAT Return.

At the end of the VAT period when the errors are discovered, the VAT account of output tax due or input tax claimed is adjusted by the net amount of all errors. The VAT account must show the amount of the adjustment being made to the VAT Return.

If more than one error is discovered in the same exercise, the net value of all the errors is used to adjust the VAT liability on the VAT Return.

Either Box 1 or Box 4 is adjusted, as appropriate. For example, if the business discovers that it did not account for VAT payable to HMRC of £100 on a supply made in the past, and also did not account for £60 VAT reclaimable on a purchase, it should add £40 to the Box 1 figure on the current VAT Return.

How to separately declare an error to HMRC: Method 2

For certain errors a separate declaration is required to the relevant HMRC VAT Error Correction Team in writing about the mistake. The simplest way to tell them is to use Form VAT 652 'Notification of Errors in VAT Returns', which is for reporting errors on previous returns, but the business does not have to use Form VAT 652 – it can simply write a letter instead.

Businesses may, if they wish, use this method for errors of any size, even those which are below the error reporting threshold ie instead of a Method 1 error correction. Using this method means the business must not make adjustment for the same errors on a later VAT Return.

Method 2 must always be used if the net error exceeds the error reporting threshold or if the errors made on previous returns were made deliberately.

Surcharges, penalties and assessments

Surcharges for missed VAT Return or VAT payment deadlines

VAT-registered businesses must submit a VAT Return and pay any VAT by the relevant due date. If HMRC receives a return or VAT payment after the due date, the business is 'in default' and may have to pay a surcharge in addition to the VAT that is owed.

The first default is dealt with by a warning known as a 'Surcharge Liability Notice'. This notice tells the business that if it submits or pays late ('defaults') again during the following 12 months – known as the surcharge period – it may be charged a surcharge.

Submitting or paying late again during the surcharge period could result in a 'default surcharge'. This is a percentage of any unpaid VAT owed. Where a correct return is not submitted at all, HMRC will estimate the amount of VAT owed and base the surcharge on that amount (this is known as an assessment – see below).

HMRC assessments

Businesses have a legal obligation to submit VAT Returns and pay any VAT owed to HMRC by the relevant due date. If they do not submit a return, HMRC can issue an assessment which shows the amount of VAT that HMRC believes it is owed, based on HMRC's best estimate.

Penalties for careless and deliberate errors

Careless and deliberate errors will be liable to a penalty, whether they are adjusted on the VAT Return or separately declared.

If a business discovers an error which is neither careless nor deliberate, HMRC expects that it will take steps to adjust or declare it, as appropriate. If the business fails to take such steps, the inaccuracy will be treated as careless and a penalty will be due.

Penalties for inaccurate returns

Penalties may be applied if a VAT Return is inaccurate, and correcting this means tax is unpaid, understated, over-claimed or under-assessed. Telling HMRC about inaccuracies as soon as the business is aware of them may reduce any penalty that is due, in some cases to zero.

Penalty for late registration

Failure to register for VAT with HMRC at the right time may make a business liable to a late registration penalty.

Penalty for failure to disclose business changes

A business which undergoes a change which either cancels the existing registration or otherwise alters the registration details will face a civil penalty if it fails to disclose the changes to HMRC within 30 days of the change.

Finding out more information about VAT

Most questions can be answered by referring to the VAT section of the HMRC website.

VAT Enquiries Helpline

If the answer to a question is not on the HMRC website, the quickest and easiest way is to ring the VAT Enquiries Helpline where most VAT questions can be answered.

Letters to HMRC

The VAT General Enquiries helpline can answer most questions relating to VAT, but there may be times when it is more appropriate to write to HMRC.

This would apply if:

- The VAT information published by HMRC - either on the website or in printed notices and information sheets - has not answered a question

- The VAT General Enquiries helpline has advised the business to write

- There is real doubt about how VAT affects a particular transaction, personal situation or business

If HMRC already publishes information that answers the question, their response will give the relevant details.

Visits by VAT officers

On a control visit to a business a VAT officer can examine VAT records to make sure that they are up to date. They also check that amounts claimed from or paid to the government are correct.